D1433361

THE MAN WHO GAVE AWAY MILLIONS

By the same Author :

THE BORROWED GARDEN
ST. JONATHAN'S IN THE COUNTRY
THE BRYDONS AT SMUGGLERS' CREEK
MORE ADVENTURES OF THE BRYDONS
THE BRYDONS GO CAMPING
THE BRYDONS DO BATTLE
THE BRYDONS IN SUMMER
SURPRISES FOR THE BRYDONS
THE BRYDONS IN A PICKLE
THE BRYDONS GET THINGS GOING
THE BRYDONS HUNT FOR TREASURE
THE BRYDONS CATCH QUEER FISH
THE BRYDONS STICK AT NOTHING
THE BRYDONS ABROAD
THE BRYDONS ON THE BROADS

TO THE WHITE NORTH
I RODE WITH THE COVENANTERS
THE WHITE-STARRED HARE
FEDORA THE DONKEY
THE STALLION FROM THE SEA
THE DROVING LAD

TALES OF THE NORTH COUNTRY
TALES OF LONDON
TALES OF THE MIDLANDS

PETE, PAM AND JIM, THE INVESTIGATORS
THE BANK HOUSE TWINS

THE DEANS MOVE IN
THE DEANS FOLLOW A CLUE
THE DEANS SOLVE A MYSTERY
THE DEANS DEFY DANGER

On the bank lay the precious package

THE
MAN WHO
GAVE AWAY MILLIONS

The story of
ANDREW CARNEGIE

KATHLEEN FIDLER

Illustrated by
HODGSON

LUTTERWORTH PRESS
LONDON

First published 1955

FOR
FRANCIS B. PINION
who encouraged me to write this book

PRINTED IN GREAT BRITAIN BY THE WHITEFRIARS PRESS LTD.
LONDON AND TONBRIDGE

Contents

Chapter		Page
1.	DUNFERMLINE DAYS	9
2.	A NEW LIFE IN A NEW WORLD	30
3.	THE TELEGRAPH BOY	51
4.	RAILWAY ADVENTURES	67
5.	CIVIL WAR IN AMERICA	87
6.	A VISIT TO SCOTLAND	97
7.	ANDREW CARNEGIE LAUNCHES OUT	111
8.	GREAT CHANGES	131
9	THE DREAM REALIZED	144

CHAPTER 1

Dunfermline Days

IT IS NOW WELL OVER A HUNDRED YEARS SINCE A VERY
small flaxen-haired boy, with quick blue eyes, ran about the
streets of Dunfermline in Scotland. There was no place
more wonderful than Dunfermline to Andrew Carnegie,
for the little city was the birthplace of Scottish history. Only
a stone's throw from his home in Moodie Street stood the
ruins of beautiful Dunfermline Abbey, founded as long ago
as 1070 by King Malcolm and his lovely Saxon queen,
Margaret. Their son, David, built the fine pillared nave
that still remains. Linked to this old nave was the restored
Abbey Church, with the tomb of King Robert the Bruce
under its central tower. Close by, in Pittencrieff Glen, was

9

all that remained of the fine royal palace where King Charles I was born. From the hill on which Dunfermline is set Andrew could see the grey waters of the Firth of Forth with the castle and spires of Edinburgh rising beyond it and behind them the blue haze of the Pentland Hills. No wonder that Andrew thought there was no more romantic place in the whole world.

The cottage in Moodie Street where he first lived was a poor simple dwelling. Downstairs was the room where William Carnegie, Andrew's father, sat at his loom and wove damask tablecloths. Upstairs was the living-room and bedroom combined, with its box-beds, built like bunks, next to the wall. Here the family both ate and slept. It was in this room that Andrew Carnegie was born in 1835, the first child of his parents.

Dunfermline was a cheerful busy place in those days, for all day the click-clack of the linen-looms could be heard in the cottages where the hand-loom weavers dwelt. At dinner-time the weavers came to their doors in their white aprons for a breath of fresh air and a gossip with each other. Weavers carrying their finished webs of cloth over their shoulders strode along the High Street to the warehouses to sell their work and bring back fresh supplies of yarn. Round the public well at the head of Moodie Street there were always one or two women having a chat while the water trickled slowly into their buckets. To all the folk of Dunfermline, coming and going, came the silvery sound of the Abbey bell, calling them to their duties through the day. From babyhood Andrew grew to know the sound of the bell and to him it always seemed a kindly voice.

Andrew's best friend was his cousin, George Lauder, whom he called " Dod " for short, and who called Andrew " Naig " (short for Carnegie) in return. Uncle Lauder kept a grocer's shop in the High Street, an enchanted place for Andrew, who loved the smell of the spices and tea, peppermint " pan-drops " and ham, and to watch the treacle oozing from a tap into a can, as he sat upon a barrel of salt-herring waiting for Uncle Lauder to finish serving a customer. When the shop was quiet in the evening, Uncle Lauder had time to tell the boys stories and teach them recitations. Then they used to put on paper helmets and, with sticks for swords, they acted the duelling scene between Norval and Glenalvon from the play *Douglas.*

" Come along, laddies, roll up your sleeves and get set at the sword fight," Uncle Lauder said. " You take your cue, Naig. ' Thou art as false——' "

Andrew squared up to Doddie with his wooden sword. " Thou art as false as——" The rest of the speech was suddenly drowned in a fit of exaggerated coughing.

" My! That's a bad cough you've got, Naig! " Uncle Lauder said with a twinkle in his eye. " You could do with a peppermint pan-drop for yon cough. Queer how it always comes on when you recite that line! "

Andrew went pink, and he and Doddie looked quickly at each other. " Now what can there be about that particular line that sets you off like that? Come along. Try again! "

" Thou art as false as——" Again Andrew was seized with a spasmodic cough.

" I doubt I'll have to say the line myself," Uncle Lauder declared, trying to keep the corners of his mouth straight. " ' Thou art as false as hell! ' "

" Oh, Uncle Lauder! " Andrew exclaimed, rather abashed. " I didn't like to say that word. It—it sounded so like swearing."

" Aye, I guessed as much," Uncle Lauder said drily. " Now, see here, Andrew. If you were to use that word by itself as an exclamation, it *would* be a swear-word, but put into a sentence like this in a play, it isn't swearing at all. There! Does that satisfy you? "

Andrew's eyes lit up. " D'you mean we can say that line without anyone telling us we're using bad words, Uncle Lauder? "

" I do, indeed? "

" Come on, then, Doddie! Lift your sword. Let's practise it *hard*! " Andrew said with tremendous satisfaction.

" All right, Naig, but we're taking turns at that part, mind! " Doddie declared, determined to have his share of that mouth-filling speech.

" ' Thou art as false as hell! ' " Naig cried, bringing out the word in a shriek of triumph, and the wooden swords clattered up and down as they fought each other over the hearth-rug.

" Did I say my part all right that time, Uncle Lauder? " Andrew demanded breathlessly.

" You were fine, Naig! Wasn't he, Father? "

" No' bad! No' bad at all! " Uncle Lauder remarked critically. " Now, Naig, let's begin at——"

Before Uncle Lauder could find the place in the book the Abbey bell began to toll.

" Mercy me, Uncle Lauder! That's not eight o'clock, is it? "

" Indeed it is, my laddie. Time you were home! You'll need to run as fast as you can if you don't want to anger your mother."

" Where's my jacket? " Andrew cried, flinging it on in a tremendous hurry. " Good-night, Uncle Lauder! Good-night, Dod! "

" Wait, now! Bide a minute, Naig," Uncle Lauder said, laying a restraining hand on Andrew's arm. " I want you to carry these two books back to your father to pass round the Reading Circle. And button your jacket up properly, lad, before you fly off as though the boggarts were after you. Which reminds me, Naig; which way are you going home to-night? "

Andrew hesitated. " Well, I usually go by the Abbey and through the kirk-yard. It's shorter."

" It'll be right dark through the kirk-yard, going by that path between the grave-stones. I'm thinking," Uncle Lauder remarked, but it seemed to Andrew there was a kind of challenge in his voice. " You'd better take the way by the May Gate to-night, where the street-lamps are shining."

Andrew still hesitated. " Uncle Lauder, do you think William Wallace would go by the May Gate or the kirk-yard? " he asked earnestly. The Scottish hero was Andrew's pattern for bravery always.

" Well, now, that's a question." Uncle Lauder stroked his head and considered gravely. He did not want Andrew to be afraid of bogeys that did not exist, but, at the same time, he did not want to test Andrew's courage beyond his strength. " It *is* a very dark night. But, of course, William Wallace was a hero."

That was enough for Andrew. " Good-night, Uncle Lauder! I'm off! " he cried, making for the shop-door before his resolution failed him.

" It's to be the May Gate, then? " Uncle Lauder called after him.

" No! The kirk-yard! "

The door banged behind him and Andrew took to his heels through the dark night. He reached the churchyard gate, and now that the street-lamps lay behind him, the path beside the Abbey looked dark indeed.

" Perhaps I'd better——" Andrew said to himself, his hand on the churchyard gate, then with staunch deliberation he said aloud, " No, I'll *not* go by the May Gate. There's nothing to scare me in the kirk-yard by day so there'll be nothing at night either. One run and I'll be through, but, please, God——" his voice trembled a little as he spoke, " please, God, don't let me trip up! " Then he plunged like a startled deer into the dark place of the sleeping dead.

Andrew was breathless when he reached the house in Edgar Street where the Carnegies lived at this time. They had moved there from Moodie Street at a time when the hand-loom weavers were well employed. Andrew flung himself up the outside stone staircase that led to the upper floor where the family lived. Below it was the workshop where his father's looms stood, silent for the night. As he burst into the living-room Mrs. Carnegie cast a glance at the clock.

"Son, you're late," she said gently.

"I'm sorry, Mother. Dod and I were play-acting with Uncle Lauder and——"

"And you forgot all about the time. I know!" His mother smiled. "Come, then, take your bread and milk and away to your bed."

Andrew cast an anxious glance at his mother. "You're not angry, are you?"

Margaret Carnegie shook her head. "No, my laddie, but next time you must watch the clock better and promise me you'll be home *before* the Abbey bell tolls eight. I know if you make a promise to me, you'll keep it." Small as he was, Andrew never broke his promises.

"Mother, do you know the Abbey bell seems to speak to me sometimes," Andrew confided. "If I've done something I shouldn't it seems to tell me so—not in an angry kind of way, but very sorry. It's a kind bell."

Mrs. Carnegie smiled at Andrew's fancy. "Perhaps you're right, Andrew, but off to bed with you, for it's high time."

Andrew said good-night and took his candle into the small room, little more than a cupboard, which opened off the living-room. Mrs. Carnegie heard the creaking of the bed that told her that Andrew was between the blankets, then she went in and blew out the candle and shut the door. As she took up her knitting again by the fireside William Carnegie said, "That's a queer notion Andrew has about the Abbey bell."

" Aye, though it's a bonnie thought for all that," Mrs. Carnegie commented. " But his head's full of whimsies. It's high time he was at the school. He's nearly eight years old now."

" Now, you remember that we both gave the lad our word that he would not be sent to the school until he asked to go."

In 1842 no child was compelled by law to attend school as children are to-day. Indeed, often poor parents could not afford the two or three pence a week that they had to pay a schoolmaster for their children's schooling.

Mrs. Carnegie pursed her lips and shook her head. " Aye, that's right enough," she agreed. " I wish, all the same, that we had not made him such a daft-like promise. Whiles it seems to me that he'll never go to school at all. Nearly eight years old and every time I mention the school, he just shakes his head and runs away. But some day he'll have to make a start."

William Carnegie stared thoughtfully into the fire. " You know what William Cobbett wrote, my lass, that the best schooling was an intelligent home, and no child should be put to school till he was eight years old. When Andrew wants to go to school cheerfully and of his own wish, then that's the time to send him."

" Cheerfully ! " Mrs. Carnegie sniffed. " He's never likely to go cheerfully when other bairns tell him tales of school-master Martin using the strap on them for not doing their lessons well ! You know what bairns are. I think Andrew's a bit feared of Mr. Martin, but if he once got to the school I'm sure he'd like his lessons."

" Aye, aye," William Carnegie agreed rather soberly. " But there's little enough money to pay the schoolmaster. There was never a time when the linen-weaving trade was so poor as it is to-day. Two or three years ago I had two men working for me. Now there's just myself, and it's hard enough to get orders for table-cloths. The factories with the newfangled machinery get all the work nowadays," he added bitterly.

Britain was importing large quantities of raw cotton from America, and this was woven into cloth in the factories, where very small children were employed. Cotton cloth made by steam-powered machinery was far cheaper than linen.

The day of the hand-loom weaver was almost over. Poverty stared men like William Carnegie in the face.

Mrs. Carnegie looked sympathetically at her husband, but she also looked very determined. " You do want Andrew to go to school, don't you, William? "

" Of course I do, lass, but it'll not be easy."

" Then he shall go ! " Margaret Carnegie declared. " It would vex me worse than anything if Andrew didn't have his chance. I know the weaving's bad just now—every linen-weaver in Dunfermline seems to have his looms standing idle—but I'll find a way somehow, you'll see, to send the boy to the school."

" There's none like you, Margaret," her husband said warmly. " But even if you do raise the money for the school, you've forgotten one thing."

" What's that? " Mrs. Carnegie asked sharply.

" That you promised the lad that you'll not send him to school till he asks to go. You can't break your promise to him, for he sets great store by promises and he's never broken one to you."

" Oh, I'm awful vexed about it ! " Mrs. Carnegie cried in exasperation. " What can we do? "

" Shall I ask Mr. Martin to speak to the lad? " his father suggested.

" No. That might put him off altogether. The school-master can be dour, as you well know."

" Aye, in the school, but when he takes the lads for an excursion to the sea, he's kind of different—not so much of

16

the schoolmaster, you understand. I hear he's taking the bairns for an outing to Inverkeithing soon."

" How would it be if you asked him to take Andrew along? If Mr. Martin talked kindly to him, the laddie would get over his fear and go to school like a shot. Maybe you could hint as much to Mr. Martin, William? "

" I'll step down and have a word with Robert Martin this very night," William promised. He was just reaching for his hat when there was a tremendous noise of shouting from the direction of the High Street.

" Whatever's that? " Mrs. Carnegie cried, her hand on her heart.

" It sounds like a riot to me! "

Running feet trampled up the outside stair to the top rooms where the Carnegies lived. There was a tapping on the window, followed by a loud knocking at the door. William Carnegie flung it open. Two men stood there.

" Is that you, William Carnegie? Your brother-in-law, Tom Morrison, has been put in the jail! "

" Oh, mercy me! What has he done? " Mrs. Carnegie exclaimed.

" It's all because of what he said at that meeting in the Abbey Pends last week, ye ken. It was a Chartist meeting and there was a lot of talk that every man should have the right to vote for a member of Parliament, and that the Corn Laws should be done away."

" Aye, but there's always been talk about such-like things. Folk have the right to speak. Surely Tom would never be put in prison for speaking his mind at a meeting? " Margaret Carnegie asked indignantly.

" It went further than that, Mrs. Carnegie. Tom Morrison recommended that the Chartists should take action this time," the second man informed her. " He was speaking at Torryburn the night."

" Action! What action? I'm sure Tom would never go

advising the crowd to throw stones and break windows and burn factories."

The door to Andrew's room opened and a frightened face peeped out.

" No, no. Morrison's a man of peace," the first man agreed. " He told us to set about getting Parliament reform by peaceful means. He told us just to stop work and stay quietly at home as other Chartists were doing all up and down the country."

" Stop work? What good would that do? " Mrs. Carnegie demanded impatiently.

" It would bring all the trade in the country to a standstill," William Carnegie declared. " It would show Parliament we meant what we said. We should refuse to work till we had our rights as citizens. It's what's called a strike, my lass."

" This is no time for arguing about rights and strikes," Margaret Carnegie declared, snatching up her shawl. " We must go to the jail at once and find out what's happening."

" Mother, don't leave me behind. I want to come too! "

" Better bring the bairn! He might get into mischief by himself at home," William Carnegie decided, and bundling Andrew into his coat he hoisted him on to his shoulder, and they all set off for the jail at the Town Hall.

It was a terrifying thing to see the angry mob at the Town Hall. They were shouting " Let Tom Morrison go free! Let Morrison out! " and they were wild with anger.

" It would take very little for them to storm the jail and carry Tom off by force," William Carnegie declared.

" Oh, I hope they'll not do that," his wife said in alarm. " It would only bring the soldiers here again to charge among the crowd with their horses and it would be worse for Tom in the end."

There had been riots before in Dunfermline when the mob had set fire to a factory—a riot that had only been quelled by the coming of the Inniskilling Dragoons who had charged the mob. Margaret Carnegie remembered that with horror.

" Wheesht, lass, there's the Provost at yon window," William said.

An angry roar from the crowd greeted the Provost's appearance, but the Provost held up his hand and asked for a hearing.

" If you'll bide quietly, Tom Morrison will speak to you himself," he declared, pointing to another window with bars.

From his father's shoulder Andrew Carnegie caught a glimpse of his uncle's rugged face flushed with excitement, his fierce brown beard and small lively eyes. He looked quite calmly at the milling crowd.

" Quiet! Let Tom Morrison speak! " Shouts came from every side and a silence gradually fell upon them as they waited for him. Many of them expected his usual fiery utterances to urge them to action, but when the words came they were quite unexpected.

" All my friends of the Chartist cause fold their arms," Morrison instructed them. Practically every member of that great crowd obeyed him.

" And now you are to walk in peace to your homes and obey the laws," he told them. In a couple of minutes he had controlled and dispersed the crowds as no argument or orders from the Provost could do. In ten minutes the streets of Dunfermline were empty and silent and the would-be rioters had gone to bed.

These were troubled times in which Andrew lived his early boyhood. The change-over to the Industrial Age, the age of steam-powered machinery was taking place, and the old craftsmen and hand-weavers were beginning to find themselves outpaced in the struggle for work. Many men were unemployed, and there was great poverty and even semi-starvation because of the high price of bread. Bread was dear partly because of poor corn harvests and partly because of the Corn Laws. These laws said that corn could not be imported from other countries until the corn grown in the British Isles reached a certain high price. It was intended to help the British farmer and make sure that he had a fair price for his labours. A sad result was that it kept the price of bread so high that the poor went hungry. Tom Morrison and the Chartists held that the Corn Laws should be abolished. Naturally these unhappy people thought that if they had a voice in the making of the laws they would be far better off. In those days not every man and woman had the right to vote to choose a member of Parliament as they have now. The Chartists thought that every man of the age of twenty-one should have a vote, and they went on strike for their rights.

Andrew took a keen interest in listening to the political arguments that went on many evenings in his own home and Uncle Tom Morrison's house, but he took an even more intense delight in the world of school. William Carnegie *did* have a talk to Mr. Martin, the schoolmaster, who invited Andrew to go with him and his scholars to Inverkeithing to picnic on the shore. Andrew discovered that out of school the schoolmaster was not nearly so terrifying a person; that he could show the boys interesting things and even talk kindly with them. He went home full of liking for Mr. Martin, and the next Monday, his face shining with well-applied soap, his coat well-brushed, though mended, and with a clean white collar, Andrew presented himself at the school in Rolland Street. Poor though they were, Mrs. Carnegie never let Andrew go to the school anything but neat and clean, always with a clean collar.

The school was just one big room heated only by a little open fire close to the door. As each child came in he would hold his hands out to the flames and rub them hurriedly, and then go to his seat and shiver for the rest of the time. Mr. Martin sat at a desk on a slightly raised platform. On the desk lay his tall hat, known as a " lum " hat in Scotland, where a chimney is called a " lum." Beside the hat was the dreaded tawse or strap which Mr. Martin never failed to use on any lazy pupils.

" I will bring it out with the tawse," he used to declare, if a pupil did not work hard enough at his lessons. For all that, Andrew, always a bright pupil, ceased to be afraid of him, and school became a world of delight, even if the schoolmaster often grimly reminded the children, " You have not been put in this world to enjoy yourself but to do your duty." For Andrew, loving to learn, duty and enjoyment were the same thing. If anything happened to prevent him from attending school, he was most unhappy.

Every day water had to be drawn from the well at the top of Moodie Street, for water was not then piped to taps in the cottages. It was Andrew's task to fetch the water before he went to school. The supply of water in the well was often just a trickle, and Andrew had to wait impatiently, hopping from one foot to the other and fearful of being late for school. Often, too, he had to wait his turn with housewives who did not mind having a gossip, or a " bit blether " as they would put it, while the water ran from the tap into their buckets. One day, when Mrs. Carnegie needed extra water for her washing, she sent Andrew on a second journey to the well.

" Oh, Mother, it's close on school-time," Andrew cried, dismayed.

" I'm sorry, laddie, but I must have the water. Your father's gone to the warehouse to see if he can get an order for table-cloths, and I cannot leave the baby."

Andrew now had a baby brother, Tom, eight years younger than himself.

" All right, Mother, I'll go," he said at once. " Only I hope I'm not kept there long."

Mrs. Carnegie peered through the window. " There are only two or three women there now. If you hurry you'll get your turn soon. I'll have your clean collar ready for you when you come back."

" Give me the bucket—I'll run ! "

At the well only two people were drawing water, Mrs Scott and Mrs. Thomson. Andrew felt very relieved and said to himself, " I'll be in time for school yet if the water's running all right."

He greeted Mrs. Scott anxiously. " Good morning, Mistress Scott. Is the water running freely ? "

" No' very fast, but it's not stopping."

" That's something to be thankful for," Andrew declared.

" Aye, but it'll take a while to fill your bucket, laddie."

Mrs. Thomson asked kindly, " Are you late for school, Andrew ? "

" Not yet. If the water runs and doesn't trickle when I get my turn I'll be in time all right."

" See, laddie, you can have my turn," Mrs. Thomson said generously, changing places with him. " Two-three minutes longer won't make any difference to me."

" That's awful good of you, Mistress Thomson ! "

" In with your bucket, then, and waste no time blethering. Here's Mrs. Ritchie coming up now."

Mrs. Ritchie made her way to the front of the little queue.

" Now, then, Andrew Carnegie, it's my turn before yours, my lad," she said blusteringly. " Make way there and shift your bucket."

" But I was here first, Mistress Ritchie," Andrew declared indignantly.

" That you may have been, but my bucket was here first, see ! " she said, pointing to the bucket which stood at the head of a line of buckets and cans and jugs.

" Your bucket! " Andrew exclaimed.

" Aye. Use your eyes, laddie. You see that line of buckets and cans? Well, they were put there last night, and there's mine the first of them all, and that gives me the right to draw my water first in the morning."

" I cannot agree with that, Mistress Ritchie," Andrew replied gravely, making no attempt to remove his bucket.

" *You* cannot! A wee bit laddie like you! " Mrs. Ritchie shrilled, red-faced. " What do you mean? "

" It's not fair and it's not right, Mrs. Ritchie. Are you telling me that if I happen to be first at the well in the morning and there's nobody here before me, I'm to sit down and wait and draw no water, all because your bucket's standing at the head of a line of cans to the well? "

" Och, don't be daft, laddie! There's nobody expects you to sit down and draw no water, because yon bucket's there."

" Well, your bucket was here to-day, but you were not, so I was quite right in drawing my water, wasn't I? " Andrew persisted.

" Maybe, so long as I wasn't here; but I'm here now and you can give me my place! "

" Aye, but I was here when you weren't here. You know, Mistress Ritchie, if you were to take it to law, I doubt if the judge would allow you were right to say a bucket could represent you at the head of the line for the well."

" Andrew Carnegie, you're as bad as your Uncle Morrison for arguing. Will you stop before you drive me clean mad? Now take that bucket of yours from under the tap."

Andrew snatched up his bucket. " Aye, Mistress Ritchie, and gladly, for my bucket's full now. You forgot the tap's been running all the time you've been talking! Good-day! "

Mrs. Ritchie stared after him. " Michty me! The young rascal! The impudence of him! " she declared.

Andrew showed in other ways, too, that he had a quick understanding of people. When his family moved to a

23

" It's all very well, Andrew Carnegie."

bigger house in Edgar Street he kept a number of pet rabbits in the little back garden, and they began to increase in number so rapidly that Andrew could not keep them in green food. He called in some of his school friends to help gather dandelions and dockens from the hedgerows. One of them, bringing back an armful of food for the rabbits, looked sideways at Andrew.

" It's all very well, Andrew Carnegie, your getting us to hunt round for food for *your* rabbits, but they don't belong to us. What are we going to get out of it for spending our Saturdays like this?" he demanded.

Andrew was nonplussed, for he had nothing to give them. Pocket-money was a thing unknown in those hard times, and sweets did not often come his way. But he was not defeated for more than a moment.

" If you'll collect food for my rabbits, I'll name the very next new rabbit after you, James."

James's face lit up. " Will you, Andrew? That's fine ! " he declared, well satisfied.

This was Andrew's first experience as an employer, but from it he learned what a strong feeling human vanity can be, and how folk will do a great deal to have their names remembered. He showed an early ability for dealing successfully with different kinds of people.

There was a time too, when Uncle Lauder found himself with a surplus of a hundred pounds of gooseberries he could not sell. He called in Dod and Naig to help him.

" Look here, laddies, if these gooseberries aren't sold to-day, then to-morrow's the Sabbath and they'll go soft over the week-end. I've more than I can sell in my shop, but could Dod and you go to Crossgates and sell them from door to door, Naig ? "

Andrew's face lit up at the thought, but he suddenly became crestfallen.

" A hundred pounds is an awful heavy weight, Uncle

Lauder. Why, it's almost as much as a sack of coal, and Crossgates is close on three miles away. Dod and I could never carry the gooseberries as far as that."

" Aye, I've thought of that, Naig. John Vick is going there with his cuddy-cart (donkey and cart) and he'll take you and the gooseberries there, if you'll go from door to door and ask for orders."

" All right, Uncle Lauder. We'll do our best," Andrew promised.

It seemed quite a big business venture for the two small boys, but at Crossgates Andrew's pleasing manners and Dod's bright smile persuaded the housewives to buy from them and they returned to Dunfermline with empty baskets.

" Well, how did you get on? " Uncle Lauder asked.

" Fine ! We've sold the whole lot, wholesale and retail, Uncle Lauder," Andrew told him proudly, as he began to count the money out.

" Well done ! " Uncle Lauder praised them. " We shall make grand business men of you yet, you'll see."

So Andrew Carnegie's schooldays ran happily by, with lessons to learn, rabbits to tend, Dod to play with, Uncle Lauder to teach them recitations and plays, and Uncle Tom Morrison to bring a spice of adventure into life with his on-goings in a world of fierce politics. But the pleasant days of learning and fun at Dunfermline were not to last very much longer. The linen-weaving trade was going from bad to worse.

" There's no more work for us at the warehouse," William Carnegie told his wife one day, after a fruitless search for orders for linen; " I doubt I shall have to sell one of the looms, my lass. Heaven knows it's almost like parting with a child, but it's stood idle long enough."

" Twenty pounds you gave for it, didn't you, William? "

He nodded miserably. " It won't fetch anything like that price now. Too many looms standing idle in Dunfermline for folk to want to buy them ! I'll be lucky if I find a purchaser."

" And what shall we do when we've spent the money that we might get for the loom? " she asked.

William shook his head. " Dear knows! "

" We can't go on like that," Margaret Carnegie decided. " We must do something before we don't know where to turn for the next shilling. William, we must leave this house. It's too big for us if you sell one of your looms, and we cannot afford the rent."

" Where shall we go then? " William asked helplessly.

" Back to Moodie Street! There's a house there with a front parlour I can turn into a shop. I can buy vegetables from the big gardens and sell them again, and I can make treacle and sugar-tablet to sell to the children at the school, and I can buy cow-heels from the butcher and boil them up and make them into moulds," she decided briskly, thinking in quick fashion of the various ways in which she could add to the family income.

" It'll be a lot of work for you, lass, and folk haven't got much money to spend."

" Better that than taking Andrew away from school." That was her one dread: that Andrew might not get the chance in life that she wanted him to have.

Margaret Carnegie was always the one to take the quick decisions; to do the practical sensible thing; to make the changes that had to be. William Carnegie could not adapt himself so well: he clung to the way of life he had always known. So long as he could work away at his loom, making his beautifully patterned damask tablecloths, humming away to himself his favourite song " The Boatie Rows," with Andrew to keep him company, he was perfectly happy. He had not the burning ambition that Margaret had for her sons; an ambition that was a driving force with her.

The loom only brought in a few shillings where it had cost pounds. A second loom was sold, and then a third. Now only one loom remained. To keep this loom going William

27

Carnegie strove desperately to obtain orders. He returned home from a visit to a buyer and as he entered the door his wife looked quickly up from her ironing.

" Were you lucky, William? " she asked.

There was no need for him to shake his head. Only too plainly his face betrayed that he had not brought home any work for his loom.

" No, lass, I was not lucky," he replied. " Mr. Mackay is not placing any more orders with hand-loom weavers. He says we take too long to deliver the goods."

" I'm sure there's no weaver could be quicker and better than you, William."

" No, wife, you're wrong there. Some can be quicker. The men who work the new-fangled looms by steam can be quicker. I begin to think the day of the hand-loom weaver is past. It's the age of machinery now. I fear there'll be little more work for the likes of us in Dunfermline."

" What's to become of us and the lads? " Mrs. Carnegie looked sober as she changed her iron at the fire.

" There's the shop, of course."

Margaret shook her head. " The shop helps to keep us clothed and respectable, but it doesn't feed us or pay the rent. Besides, what about Andrew and Tom? What kind of work is there going to be for them in Dunfermline? "

" I can't tell you. Perhaps something will come along for them," William Carnegie said vaguely.

"William, it's no use *waiting* for something to come along ! You've got to go looking for good fortune, not wait till it comes knocking at your door. I know what we'll do. We'll sell the loom and the furniture. We'll have an auction sale."

William looked at her bewildered. " But if you sell the loom, you sell our only way of making a living."

" Oh, no, we don't ! With the money we'll get from the sale we'll make a fresh start," his wife planned.

" A fresh start? Where? "

"In America! We'll go to my sisters in Pittsburgh. I had a letter from Kitty only to-day saying how well she and Tom Hogan were doing now. It's the same with Anna. She says they are putting money by, and William's farm is prospering. They've asked us many a time to go to them. Let us sell up here and go."

William looked at her sadly. "But won't it break your heart to leave Dunfermline, Margaret?"

"It would break it more to see my two boys growing up without a trade in their fingers. The day of the hand-loom weaver is past; you said it yourself, William."

William Carnegie made a little deprecating gesture with his hand.

"It's no use, William," she went on. "Let's face it squarely. We've no money to pay for the lads to be apprenticed to any other trade. But in America two honest hard-working boys would not be long in making their own way. Andrew, now, he's as sharp as a needle. He'll do well in America, you'll see."

William Carnegie sat silently for a minute or two, then sadly he nodded.

"Very well, Margaret, we'll go to America, if you think it will be best for us all. But we'll have sore hearts parting with Dunfermline and all our friends here." Then brightening up as a thought struck him, "Maybe there'll be work for hand-loom weavers in America!"

Mrs. Carnegie seemed about to remark on this, then abruptly she pursed her lips together, and looked at him with understanding, pitying eyes, almost as if he were one of the children.

"I'll make a spoon or spoil a horn!" she said almost to herself. Porridge spoons in Scotland were made of horn, and by this she meant that she was determined to make or break the Carnegies in this venture to the new land overseas.

29

CHAPTER 2

A New Life in a New World

IT WAS NOT REALLY SURPRISING THAT THE CARNEGIES should decide to go to America. It was an age of emigration. Many Scots who could not find sufficient work in their homeland went across the Atlantic to the new country where there was employment and opportunity for all, a land of promise and rich rewards for those who were not afraid of hard work. The tide of settlement rolled steadily across the prairies to the Rocky Mountains, and over the Rockies to the blue shores of the Pacific.

Already several members of the Morrison family had made their homes in America and were doing well. Margaret's two sisters, Kitty and Anna (Mrs. Hogan and Mrs. Aitken respectively) had settled in Allegheny, near Pittsburgh in Pennsylvania. William Morrison had a fine farm in Ohio. It was small wonder that when their letters arrived in Dunfermline, Margaret Carnegie was envious of their opportunities, and hoped for equal chances for Andrew and Tom.

So the decision was made to go to America, and the loom and the furniture were sold. The loom fetched a very poor price indeed and the furniture did very little better. To her dismay Mrs. Carnegie found herself twenty pounds short of the sum needed to take her family to America. She went to buy bread from her friend, Mrs. Henderson, who kept a little shop in Edgar Street, next door to where the Carnegies used to live. Mrs. Henderson was her life-long friend. She, too, was the wife of a weaver, and when the hard times came she had helped the family income by opening a small shop and baking and selling bread. From this small beginning her baker's business grew and prospered, so that the Hendersons were able to save ten shillings a month towards buying their house.

" How did the sale go, Meg? " Ailie Henderson asked. To her surprise tears sprang into Mrs. Carnegie's eyes.

" We've sold all, Ailie, and it's still not enough."

" Not enough? "

" Not enough to pay our fares to America! We'll be forced to bide in Dunfermline after all," Mrs Carnegie told her, bitterly disappointed.

" How much are you short? " Ailie Henderson asked practically.

" Twenty pounds."

Mrs. Henderson was silent for a minute as she popped the loaf into Mrs. Carnegie's basket. Then suddenly she said, " I'll help you, Meg. I'll lend it to you."

" What? Twenty pounds, Ailie? No, no, you cannot do that," Mrs. Carnegie cried. " It's a great amount of money."

" We've got just the twenty pounds put by. We've been saving it little by little towards buying our own house. It's taken three years."

" No, no! I couldn't take it. Times may be hard again and you'll need it, Ailie. But you're a true friend to offer it," said Mrs. Carnegie, her eyes brimming with tears.

" No, take it, Meg. It's as safe with you as it is with me. You can pay me back when you're doing well in America."

" But it means you putting off owning your own home," Margaret protested.

" Not for long. We haven't enough saved up, anyway. Maybe by the time you're in a good position in America and can pay me, we'll have saved enough by then. Go on, Meg, it's only like putting the money from one pocket to another."

" But suppose I never did pay you back? " Margaret asked. " We've our way to make in America, you know. It might take a long time."

" I trust you and I'm willing to wait," Mrs. Henderson said simply.

So Margaret Carnegie took Mrs. Henderson's generous loan to help to pay their passages across the Atlantic. It is a strange thing to think that but for the trust and kindness of this good friend there might have been no chances for the Carnegies in America; no acquiring of great wealth, no lavish spending of millions of money later on for the benefit of mankind. We, as well as the Carnegies, owe a debt of gratitude to Ailie Henderson. Without her timely help there might be now no Carnegie libraries nor other great benefits. On one generous action so many fortunes turned.

Another equally generous gift helped the Carnegies on their travels, too. When William's sister, Charlotte Drysdale, came to say good-bye to him, she put two golden sovereigns in his hand and a ten-shilling piece.

" That's for you," she said quietly.

William knew that she was little better off than he was.

" But where did you get this, Lottie? " he stammered.

" It's my Society money. I withdrew it from the funds."

The " Society " was a Sick and Burial Club to which the weavers subscribed a few pence a week, almost like an insurance society.

William was so moved by her generosity that he could hardly find words, and the tears filled his eyes.

" If ever I have anything in America, I'll remember you," he told her.

On the 17th day of May, 1848, the Carnegies left Dunfermline. William Carnegie was then forty-three years old, his wife ten years younger, Andrew thirteen, and his brother Tom five. They left in the horse-drawn omnibus that ran

upon the coal road down to Charleston on the shores of the
Firth of Forth; from there they were to take the steamer
across the estuary to Edinburgh. William Carnegie was in
deep grief at the thought of leaving Dunfermline and his
fellow weavers. Andrew was no less grief-stricken. He stood
at the end of the omnibus watching the roofs and towers of
the city disappear over the crest of the hill. He fixed his eyes
on the grand old Abbey and the four-square Abbey Tower
with the stone letters round it KING ROBERT THE BRUCE, as
the morning sun shone upon it.

" Oh, when shall I see you again? " he cried aloud, and
burst into tears.

All the years of his life the little grey city of his birth was
to hold a warm place in his heart, and his longing for it was
never forgotten. When he became wealthy he gave many
gifts to Dunfermline for the benefit of the folk there, especially the boys and girls. It was in Dunfermline that the first
Carnegie Free Library was built many years later.

A rowing boat took the party to the ferry steamer. Uncle
Lauder, Doddie and Uncle Tom Morrison going to see
them safe on board. As they were about to pass on to the
steamer Andrew suddenly turned and flung his arms about
Uncle Lauder.

" I cannot leave you ! I cannot leave you ! " he cried.

Though Uncle Lauder, the tears starting in his kind blue
eyes, tried to release Andrew's arms from his neck, Andrew
was gripping him so tightly that he could not loosen him. A
kindly sailor came to Uncle Lauder's assistance. " Come,
my laddie, come ! " he said, and managed to tear him away
from his dearly-beloved uncle. " Up on to the deck with
you, now ! " and he heaved Andrew bodily on to the deck
of the steamer.

The Carnegies' journey was almost entirely by water, for
this was the cheapest method of travelling then. The first
part was in very slow motion indeed, on a horse-drawn barge

to Glasgow along the Forth and Clyde Canal. Once they were on the barge Andrew's tears dried, and he began to look about him with tremendous interest as they wound their way through busy little towns, for he had never been further than Edinburgh before. The trip by barge took them two days, and on May 19 they reached the Broomielaw. Here the ship was docked that was to take them to America, the *Wiscassett,* a square-rigged schooner of eight hundred tons. Though by this time steamships were making the voyage across the Atlantic regularly, the Carnegies could not afford the higher fares demanded. That was why they decided to go by sailing ship, which carried cargo and a few passengers. There was no time, nor money, even to see Glasgow before they sailed. With a fair following wind the *Wiscasset* left the Clyde for the rougher seas beyond.

The voyage took seven weeks. It must often have been a weary time for Mrs. Carnegie, trying to wash her sons' shirts in a bucket of salt water, and sleeping in cramped wooden bunks below decks, but Andrew loved every minute of it. He had a genius for making romance out of everything, and found friends easily. Before long he was learning the names of the ropes and their purposes, and he made himself useful to the seamen by carrying messages, and helping with the work connected with the passengers.

" Andrew, you're a useful laddie," the boatswain remarked one day. " I think we'll have to make you one of the crew—a kind of cabin-boy! Well, the crew get plum-pudding for their dinner on Sundays, so you're invited to join us for Sunday dinner."

This was a rare treat for Andrew. He gratefully accepted, and Sunday always found him seated among the sailors for his dinner, next to Robert Barryman if possible, for of all the crew he was Andrew's favourite.

To the small fair-haired boy the bustle and noise of New York seemed overwhelming, used as he was to Dunfermline's slower pace. For all that, while waiting for the boat that was to take them to Pennsylvania Andrew managed to find his way around, and learned quite a lot about the ways of the new country. It was while he was walking around on one of these short excursions to explore the city that someone suddenly caught hold of him from behind and lifted him off his feet.

" Hullo, youngster, is this how you spend your time now? " he cried. It was Robert Barryman, Andrew's sailor hero. He was wearing dazzling white trousers and a blue jacket with brass buttons. Andrew thought he looked very splendid indeed. " How are you liking New York? " he asked.

" I've never seen any place like it before," Andrew admitted, both tactfully and truthfully.

" Have you tasted sarsaparilla yet? " the sailor asked. Andrew shook his head. There was no money in the Carnegie purse for novelties.

" Come over there to that refreshment stand, then."

The refreshment stand was kept by an old woman who drew a glass of sarsaparilla from a highly ornamented brass fountain which looked very gorgeous to Andrew. The sarsaparilla was a sweet syrupy drink made from the roots of certain plants. Andrew had never tasted anything like it before : to him it was like nectar. In all his long years in America he never forgot the taste of that " soda fountain " type of drink, nor the the kindness of Robert Barryman to a small boy. Andrew possessed strongly the fine quality of gratitude, and he always tried to repay any kindness. In later years he tried to trace Robert Barryman to see if he could make his old age more comfortable, but he was nowhere to be found.

Along the Erie Canal by way of Buffalo and Lake Erie, then down the canal again to Beaver City; the journey took three weeks then by the slow and not over-clean canal barge

—to-day it takes only a few hours by rail. From Beaver City a steamboat would take them up the Ohio river to Pittsburgh. The worst part of the journey occurred when they had to spend the night on the canal-boat at Beaver waiting for the steamboat to arrive. Clouds of mosquitoes invaded the cabins, the poor travellers were very severely bitten, and Mrs. Carnegie suffered the worst of all.

" Oh, mercy me, just look at us ! " she exclaimed. " We're covered with bites and I'm the worst. The skin round my eyes is so puffed up I can hardly see out of them. A fine sight to greet Kitty and Anna in Pittsburgh ! Why, they'll not know me ! Shall we have this bother with mosquitoes every night, William ? "

William shook his head. " I think it'll be better when we reach running water, my lass. For all that, the laddies slept pretty soundly."

" A good thing they did ! But Andrew runs up and down so much looking at everything, that it's not to be wondered that he's fast asleep whenever his head touches the pillow."

The burdens and discomforts of their travels were soon forgotten in the warmth of the welcome they received at Pittsburgh from the Hogans and the Aitkens. Kitty Hogan and Anna Aitken, Mrs. Carnegie's twin sisters, had already been eleven years in America. To them it seemed as if the Carnegies brought with them the breath of Scotland indeed. They lost no time in taking William and Margaret and the boys to their new home in Allegheny City, adjoining Pittsburgh.

Allegheny was a rough, ready-made kind of town of " frame " or wooden houses, which had grown very quickly. It straggled along a muddy bank of the river and was the home of many miners and ironworkers. Rebecca Street, where the Hogans lived, was one of the muddiest of streets, down by the water-front. Whenever the river overflowed, the street was flooded. Andrew and Tom rather enjoyed this, but you may be sure Mrs. Carnegie did not, for she loved to keep her home spotless.

Aunt Aitken, who was a widow, had a little grocery store, Uncle Thomas Hogan, who was a clerk in a crockery shop, had a small two-storied frame house. Behind the house, and built on to it, was another dwelling of two rooms. The lower one was occupied by a weaver's loom, and the upper room became the Carnegies' home. Thomas Hogan's brother, Andrew, had worked the loom, but he had given up hand-loom weaving for more profitable work. William Carnegie immediately set to work to weave chequered damask table-cloths just as he had done in Dunfermline! Unfortunately he could find no dealer in linen goods to sell his table-cloths for him, and he had to turn pedlar and sell them from door to door, and he got very little money from them indeed. That was the sad thing about William Carnegie. He could not adapt himself to the changing conditions of the new world. He just could not get used to the machine age, nor take part in it.

Difficulties only brought out the fighting spirit in Margaret Carnegie. In her father's shoemaker's shop in Dunfermline, she had learnt to bind shoes. She went to see Henry Phipps, a shoemaker in Rebecca Street, who was also a Scot.

" Good-morning, Mr. Phipps. I am sister to Mrs. Hogan," she announced.

" Aye, we've heard a lot about your coming to America. I hope you like it here."

" We shall like it well enough if we can make a living," Mrs. Carnegie told him in her blunt straightforward manner. " But my boys are young yet and we shall all need to work. I have come to see if you have any work for *me*."

" It's not often one hears of a woman making shoes," Henry Phipps told her. " It's a skilled occupation, you know. It's got to be learnt first."

" My father and brother were shoemakers and I used to bind shoes for them from being a bit lassie. I could bind shoes for you. I want work to do in my own home."

" Well, my lass, I'll give you a trial. If you can bind shoes to my satisfaction you could earn four dollars a week." Four dollars a week was worth about sixteen shillings in those days. Although it may seem rather poor wages, money could buy much more then than it does now.

Mrs. Carnegie's wage would at least help to keep the family in food, but it was not enough, and William's earnings from his hand-woven table-cloths would not bring in very much. Tom, being only five years old, went to school; but there was still Andrew. Thirteen-year-old Andrew began to look round for work.

Midnight often found Mrs. Carnegie at her shoe-binding. In addition to her work for Mr. Phipps, she managed to keep her home and children bright and clean and to cook and wash for them. Often in the evenings Andrew and Tom would try to help her by waxing threads and threading needles, and she would recite to Tom and tell him tales of Scotland. Sometimes, when she and Andrew were alone, they would figure out ways and means. Andrew had been searching for a job but so far had not been lucky.

" I wish you could have continued your education, Andrew," Mrs. Carnegie said regretfully one evening.

" And I wish I could find a job so *you* didn't have to work so hard," Andrew told her. " But employers look at me and say ' You're awful small ', and they don't seem to believe I'm thirteen."

" Cheer up, laddie ! Something will come along yet."

" I've been figuring it out. If we could raise twenty-five dollars a month—that's about five pounds—say twenty-five shillings a week, could you manage with that ? " Andrew asked his mother with a seriousness far older than his years.

" Yes, I think I could. But I'd like to have a little money

over so that I could put a bit by to pay Ailie Henderson the twenty pounds I owe her," Mrs. Carnegie said soberly. The thought of the unpaid debt was constantly with her. So far, since coming to America, they had been little better off than when they left Dunfermline.

" Then I've just *got to* find some work," Andrew said with grim determination.

Just then Andrew Hogan, Aunt Kitty's brother-in-law, called in to see them. They asked him if he knew of any work for Andrew.

" What do you want to do, my lad? " he asked Andrew.

" I'd work at anything honest."

" That's the spirit, laddie. You're a likely lad and apt at learning."

" Andrew would work hard, Mr. Hogan. Do you know of anything for him, now? " Mrs. Carnegie asked anxiously.

Andrew Hogan stroked his chin. " Well—no. I can't say I know of any actual post. Have you ever thought of fitting the lad out with a pedlar's basket, pins and buttons and tapes, bootlaces and socks and the like, and sending him round the wharves to sell them among the barge-folk there? I don't say he'd make a fortune, but he'd do pretty well out of it."

Mrs. Carnegie looked horrified. " Are you serious, Andrew Hogan? What! My son a pedlar going among all the rough characters upon the wharves? Surely not! "

" Don't take my suggestion unkindly, Mistress Carnegie. I still thinks it's quite a good idea, seeing there's no other work for him," Andrew Hogan persisted, but Mrs. Carnegie looked so annoyed that he decided he had better leave her to think it over.

" Well, I want to see Tom and Kitty, so I'll just slip next door. Good-night to you," he said.

The minute the door closed behind him, Mrs. Carnegie burst into tears : " Oh, to think that we have sunk so low that there's no better job for my boy than being a pedlar! "

Andrew put his arm about her. " Don't, Mother, don't! " he begged. " This is not like you. Take heart! Something's bound to turn up. It must! But don't weep, please. I can't bear to see you weep."

" It's all right now," Mrs. Carnegie said, drying her eyes quickly, ashamed to have given way to tears and afraid lest she should have upset Andrew too. " Don't mind my foolishness, laddie. I just couldn't bear the thought that I had brought you all the way to America just to become a pedlar —a going-about body, with no real trade in your fingers. I'd made such grand dreams about what you and Tom would do in this fine new land."

" Don't be feared, Mother. I'll make your dreams come true, see if I don't! " Andrew said stoutly. " I'll see that you ride in your carriage yet, the finest lady in the land."

Mrs. Carnegie could not help laughing, not at Andrew's dream, but at the picture of herself as a fine lady riding in a carriage.

" Nay, nay, Andrew! What kind of fine lady would I make? " She shook her head a little sadly. " And what good would it do me to ride in a carriage if the folk of Dunfermline couldn't see me? "

" I'll *make* it come true. I will! "

" No, my laddie, I'll be satisfied to see you a useful man in the world, honoured and respected, and doing always what is right."

" I'll do my best," Andrew promised, but from then on he locked his dream in his heart : that his mother should some day ride through the streets of Dunfermline in her own carriage.

When William Carnegie found there was little sale for his table-cloths he was forced to seek work elsewhere, and he took a job in a cotton-weaving factory belonging to an old Scotsman, Mr. Blackstock. William asked if there was any work for Andrew too, and Mr. Blackstock offered him a job as bobbin boy at one dollar and twenty cents a week, then worth about five shillings. It was little enough, but at least Andrew felt it was something to help his mother.

It was a hard life. Father and son rose while it was still dark and began work at six in the morning, and they finished work at six o'clock at night. There was no law about an eight-hour day in the factories then. It was Andrew's job to fill the bobbins or reels with yarn for the weavers, and all day he sat at the bobbin wheel. It was irksome work for a boy with imagination, a boy who wanted to use his mind as well as his hands, but Andrew stuck it out because, he said later, " It gave me the feeling I was doing something for my world—our family. I have made millions since, but none of those millions gave me such happiness as my first week's earnings. I was now a helper of the family, a breadwinner."

Andrew stayed at the factory longer than his father did. William could not endure the factory life and was so unhappy in it that he was soon back at his own hand-loom again, making his table-cloths and singing away as he worked the treadles. Andrew was unhappy too, perhaps most of all at being separated from his father, for he had taken great joy in joining his father at the loom and singing with him.

Shortly after this Andrew was offered work in a factory that made the bobbins used in the cotton mills. Mr. John Hay, the factory owner, was willing to pay Andrew two dollars a week. This seemed such a good rise in pay that Andrew accepted the new post at once. On arrival at his work Mr. Hay took him to the boiler house in the cellar of the factory where Andrew was to work.

" Now, my lad, you see that small steam-engine? It'll be your job to keep the boiler fire going and the steam-engine working. You'll need to watch the steam gauges all the time, mind! If you run too big a head of steam you might burst the boiler, and if you let the fires too low, the workers in the factory above will complain they're not getting power enough to run their lathes. So try to keep the steam pressure even. Never take your eyes off the gauges, my lad, and keep the fire steadily stoked. You're small built. Do you think you can manage it? " Mr. Hay looked a little doubtful.

" I'll do my best, sir."

" Well, the job's worth two dollars a week if you do your work properly."

Andrew set to work to keep the boiler fire stoked. As he did so the pulsing steam engine seemed to say, " Two dollars a week! Two dollars a week! " When the steam pressure dropped too low, the engine rumbled, " Two dollars a week! Two dollars a week! " in a slightly menacing tone, as though doubting whether Andrew would ever earn it. It was worse, though, when the pressure rose too high, for then it would shriek at him in rising tones, " Two dollars a week! Two dollars a week! " till it became a threat and Andrew became afraid the boiler would blow himself and it up altogether.

For a boy who loved to work with other people, it was a lonely unhappy job, but whenever he felt like giving it up he thought of his mother and what the extra two dollars meant to the family income. The constant stoking of the boiler was hard work for a small lad whose muscles were not yet toughened, and he felt tired out at the end of each day's work. Not for a moment would he have complained though, and given his parents cause for worry. Always he watched the sinister steam gauges, rising and falling, rising and falling, until he began to have nightmares about them.

One night he sat up in bed, perspiring with the terrors of his dream.

" Watch the gauges! Watch the gauges! " he shouted. " The pressure's sinking too low and I can't get power for the workers. Oh! Oh! I can't get the steam up! I can't get the steam up! Fling on the coal! Watch the gauges! Watch the gauges! Now they are going too high. The boiler'll burst! The boiler'll burst!"

Tom, lying in bed beside Andrew, sat up and began to shake him.

"Andrew! Andrew! What's the matter? You're shouting in your sleep. What's wrong?"

"It's the gauges!" Andrew cried, still half-asleep and dreaming he was stoking the boiler. "They keep flying up and then sinking down. What shall I do? What shall I do?"

Tom shook him harder still. "Wake up, Andrew! Wake up! You're having a nightmare. Michty me! What are you talking about?"

"Oh, Tom, I must have been dreaming," Andrew said. "It's the boiler and the gauges. I'm awful feared I'll do something daft and smash yon boiler at the factory."

"You're always crying out in your sleep," Tom told him. "If you do it any more, I shall tell my mother."

"Oh, no, you mustn't! Give me your word you won't," Andrew begged his small brother. "This job means two dollars a week to my mother. She's got enough troubles without having to worry about me. You're not to say anything, now. I can stick it till something better turns up."

Perhaps Mr. Hay realized that stoking a boiler all day and keeping a level pressure of steam was too much for the rather under-sized lad; perhaps he was moved by a wish to help along a younger brother Scot; but one day he sent a bigger lad to take Andrew's place and called Andrew up to the office.

"Go wash your hands, first, my lad," he directed Andrew.

Andrew made frantic endeavours to remove most of the coal-dust from his hands under a cold water tap. Then he presented himself to Mr. Hay again.

"You can write, can't you?"

43

" Yes, sir."

" A good hand, now? "

" Yes, I think so, sir."

" Then write out a bill-head for me so I can see what kind of writing you do."

Andrew copied a bill-head in his very best copper-plate writing that Mr. Martin in Dunfermline had taught him. Mr. Hay grunted approval.

" Right, Andrew! You can make out my bills for me. I suppose you're good at figures too? "

" Oh, yes, sir! " Andrew replied with more confidence than modesty.

" Well, then, that's to be your job now, but it won't take all your time writing bill-heads for me," the canny Scot said. " I must find you another job to fill in the time. You can run messages for me, and you can bathe the new-made bobbins in the oil vats."

So to Andrew fell the very nauseating task of bathing the new spools in evil-smelling oil. The oil clung to his fingers, and the smell of it always seemed to be about his clothes. It turned his stomach and many times he had to rush away to be sick. Though he never overcame the horrible feeling of sickness he kept on with his task, determined he would never give in.

The other side of his work for Mr. Hay, the office work, held a great deal of interest for him. Mr. Hay discovered that Andrew was quite truthful in saying he was good at figures, and he began to let Andrew look after his account books too. Mr. Hay kept his books in a simple fashion known as single entry. Andrew had heard that big firms kept their account books in what was called double entry, a different system of book-keeping. He talked about this to his great friends in Rebecca Street, John Phipps, son of the shoemaker, and Thomas Miller.

" I think in double entry each item is put down twice

under different headings in an account book." John Phipps said rather vaguely. "The second entry is a check on the first."

" Where can I find out about it? " Andrew demanded.

" There's a Mr. Williams teaches book-keeping at a night-school in Pittsburgh during the winter."

" Then let's *all* go to him," Andrew said at once.

All the boys were anxious to get on and become more proficient in their work, so they all attended the night-school and learned double entry book-keeping. Andrew was indeed serving his apprenticeship to the wide business-life that was to lie before him.

He continued to work for Mr. Hay till he was nearly fifteen. Then one of those sudden chances occurred that can alter the course of a whole life. Uncle Hogan was very fond of a game of draughts, or checkers, as it is called in America. One evening he was playing against Mr. David Brooks, the manager of the newly-opened telegraph office in Pittsburgh. The telegraph had been invented only about ten years earlier, and it was still quite a new thing in America.

" How's the telegraph business doing, Mr. Brooks? " Thomas Hogan asked at the conclusion of the game.

" Wonderfully, man, wonderfully! More and more people are sending messages by it every day. The business men in Pittsburgh and the railway people are finding out how useful it is to them. My messenger boy is kept running up and down the streets all day delivering telegrams. There's really too much work for one lad. I'll have to find another."

" Will you now? " Mr. Hogan said thoughtfully.

" Yes, I could do with one. You don't happen to know of a lad who might suit, do you, Hogan? "

" Aye, I know a boy who might do; he's a thought on the small side, maybe, but he's a quick honest lad. He's my nephew, Andrew Carnegie. He's working for Mr. Hay the bobbin manufacturer just now, but I think he's looking for something better."

" What wages does he get with Mr. Hay, do you know? "

" Two dollars a week," Mr. Hogan told him.

" Mm!! Well, if he's suitable, the job with me would be worth two-and-a-half dollars a week. Tell him to come and see me right away if he's interested."

Andrew was wild with delight when he heard of the possibility of a new job at higher pay, away from the sickening oil vats—a new job that would take him out and about, meeting all kinds of people. He decided to see Mr. Brooks at once, and his mother agreed with him. His father, however, was always slower to come round to an idea, and he had many doubts about the wisdom of such a move.

" The lad's doing well enough where he is," he said.

Andrew almost danced with impatience. " But Mr. Brook's wage is two-*and-a-half* dollars a week, Father. Think of it! Half a dollar a week rise! "

Mr. Carnegie shook his head. " But you're too young and too small for a job like that, Andrew."

" Only give me a chance at it and you'll see! "

" I don't think for one minute you'll get it. For all that money Mr. Brooks will be expecting a far bigger boy. You'd better stay in the job you've got."

Andrew's face fell. " Oh, Father, let me go and see Mr. Brooks at least," he begged.

Mrs. Carnegie always believed in seizing opportunities too, and she sympathized with Andrew. " Let the lad go, William," she urged.

" Suppose he was sent far out into the country late at night with a message? The telegraph office is open late, you know."

" Och! I'd manage all right, Father. I'm not afraid," Andrew said.

" It could do no harm for the lad to ask Mr. Brooks about the situation," Mrs. Carnegie put in.

" But suppose he doesn't get it and he loses his present job in the bargain? "

46

" Mr. Hay is a decent body. Surely he'd keep it open for Andrew? Couldn't you go and ask him, William? I don't think he'd stand in the boy's way of getting on in the world."

William Carnegie did consult Mr. Hay, who was fair-minded enough to say that the chance of the new situation might be to Andrew's advantage, and he generously offered to keep his old job open for him if Mr. Brooks turned him down.

The next day Andrew and his father walked the two miles to Pittsburgh. Mrs. Carnegie saw to it that Andrew looked very smart indeed. He wore a clean white linen shirt and his best navy-blue jacket and trousers. He had scrubbed his face and brushed his hair well. As they went along Andrew decided that he was going to obtain the post entirely by himself. He did not want his father to go into the telegraph office with him and express any blundering doubts of Andrew's fitness for the post, even to pointing out that he was rather small! When they reached the telegraph office at the corner of Fourth Street and Wood Street, Andrew suddenly halted.

" I want to go in by myself, Father, *please,*" he said urgently. " Will you wait here for me? "

Something in Andrew's voice and face made William Carnegie consent, though it was almost against his better judgment, and Andrew climbed the stairs alone. He was directed to Mr. Brooks's office.

" Please, sir, I'm Andrew Carnegie. I've come about the post of telegraph boy. My uncle, Mr. Hogan, sent me," he introduced himself.

Mr. Brooks looked kindly but doubtfully at him. " Mm! You're smaller than I thought! "

" Please, sir, I'm still growing."

Mr. Brooks smiled a little. " Yes, you're small, but maybe you're wiry. Do you know the streets of Pittsburgh well? "

Andrew felt it was better to be completely honest. " No,

47

" I've come about the post of telegraph boy."

sir, I don't. My home is in Allegheny, two miles away."

"Well, you're straightforward, at any rate," Mr. Brooks commented, but he looked undecided. "All the same, I must have a boy who knows every street in Pittsburgh; yes, and all the business firms, too. Telegraph messages have to be delivered with speed, you know."

"I could learn, sir," Andrew said eagerly. "I'd do my best to learn quickly. Will you please give me a trial?"

Mr. Brooks smiled at him. "You're keen to have the job, aren't you, my lad? If I did say I would give you a trial, when could you start?"

"Right now, sir!"

"Now? This minute?" Mr. Brooks looked rather surprised at Andrew's quick decision.

"Right away! At once, sir! That's if you'll let me, Mr. Brooks."

"Well, if you learn your way about Pittsburgh as quickly as you make up your mind, you'll soon have the job at your fingers' ends. Very well, Andrew, I'll give you a trial. You can go along with George McLain, the other telegraph boy, for a day or two till you've found your way round. You can start right away, to-day. The wages are two-and-a-half dollars a week."

"Thank you, sir," Andrew said gratefully. "I feel I'm really getting a start in life. Please may I run down to the corner of the street before I begin work?"

"Yes, but why?"

"To tell my father I've got the job, sir. He's waiting to hear how I get on. I'll come straight back."

Andrew sped down the stairs as though his feet had wings. On the way he passed George McLain, returning from taking a message. William Carnegie was still waiting on the kerb-stone. Andrew grasped him by the arm.

"Father, I've got the job! I'm starting work *now,* this minute!" he cried excitedly. "Will you go home and tell

Mother, please? And tell her I'll be bringing home two-and-a-half dollars a week. Why, that's about ten shillings!" His new wages seemed riches indeed to the Carnegies.

When George McLain arrived in the office Mr. Brooks told him, "I've just appointed another telegraph boy to assist you, George. I want you to take him round with you for a day or two and show him the ropes."

George McLain looked slightly disgusted. "Was that the wee chap I saw on the stairs just now?"

"Aye, that's Andrew Carnegie."

"How's such a little fellow going to manage this job? He's too small."

"Well, we'll see how he goes on. Do your best to help him. You'll find he's willing to learn," Mr. Brooks told him.

CHAPTER 3

The Telegraph Boy

ANDREW LIKED HIS NEW JOB IMMENSELY. IT WAS SO different from his work in the hot cellar, shovelling coal, watching the gauges and alone all the time. It was far better even than his work for Mr. Hay at the bobbin factory, for now he was free at last from the horrible smell of the oil vat. Most of his work was out-of-doors, and how he re-velled in the sunshine! He enjoyed the running hither and thither with the telegrams and meeting many new people whom he soon learned to recognize when he met them on the street. He was so determined to learn the various busi-ness houses in Pittsburgh that he made notes of them all, up one side of a street and then down the other. Whenever he had a minute to spare, and in the evenings, he named the streets and then recited the names of the firms in the correct order. He certainly kept his word to Mr. Brooks that he would learn his way about quickly. Not only did he learn the names of the different businesses, but he tried to remem-ber the men who were at the head of them. By his quick recognition he was often able to deliver a message to a man when he met him on the street, thus saving valuable time. He was often praised for his quickness in delivering messages.

Sometimes Andrew received little gifts when he delivered a telegram; apples from the fruiterer; cakes from the baker; and even an occasional tip. All these he took home to share with his mother and father and Tom.

Pittsburgh in 1850 was largely a wooden city : only one

or two of the houses and business premises were built of brick. There was, however, a theatre, which was to play a part in Andrew's life very soon. Pittsburgh was a coal-mining town with growing pig-iron manufactures. Every day a steamer arrived from Cincinnati along the Ohio River, and goods were transferred to it from the canal which linked Pittsburgh with the east, so the city was rapidly growing as a transfer and forwarding centre to all the surrounding countryside. The telegraph business grew with the city. The work of the Eastern Telegraph Company expanded so much that another telegraph boy was appointed, David McCargo, who also came of Scottish parents. The two boys became close friends and their friendship lasted a lifetime. Before long Mr. Brooks asked Andrew to name two other boys for messengers, and, of course, he chose his own friends from the little Scottish colony in Rebecca Street. Robert Pitcairn and Henry Oliver joined the telegraph company. There was great excitement among them when James Reid, the super-intendent of the telegraph line, was to pay the office a visit, for he was a Scot too. All the boys were lined up for his inspection in the main office.

" Aye, aye, you're five clean well-set-up laddies," Mr. Reid said with some satisfaction, for there was a clannish feeling among the Scots, and every one of them tried to help along a brother Scot in the New World.

"Yon wee chap ! " He pointed to Andrew. " Where do you hail from in Scotland ? "

" Dunfermline, sir."

" I'm a Dunfermline man myself," Mr. Reid said with a smile and a nod. " And you're doing well as a telegraph boy, I hope."

" Andrew's one of our smartest lads," Mr. Brooks said. " Though they are all hard workers."

" Aye, there's only one fault I have to find with them," Mr. Reid said. The boys waited rather fearfully to know what this was. "They're all dressed differently," Mr. Reid went on; "one in navy and another in grey, one with a scarf and another without. They would all look better wearing the same uniform."

"I doubt if the boys could afford it——" Mr. Brooks was beginning in a low voice, but Mr. Reid interrupted him.

"The telegraph company's doing very well, very well indeed. It can afford to provide a uniform for its messengers. Now, boys, cut along to Cohen's the tailor's shop, and ask him to measure you all for a uniform, jackets and knickerbockers, and to send patterns of a hard-wearing dark green cloth to Mr. Brooks, for him to select what is most suitable."

The boys were all delighted at their new magnificence, especially Andrew. The uniform gave them a team spirit and it made them proud to serve the telegraph company. They became very well-known figures in Pittsburgh as they darted up and down the streets, and were proud to be recognized by many of the leading business men.

The telegraph company delivered messages free to Mr. Foster, the manager of the Pittsburgh theatre, who gave the company a number of free tickets to see the plays. It was often Andrew's job to deliver the telegrams to the theatre. If this happened during the early evening, Mr. Foster would sometimes wink at Andrew and jerk his thumb upwards, which meant that Andrew could climb the stairs to the gallery and take one of the unoccupied seats there.

In this way Andrew made his first acquaintance with Shakespeare. This was a great delight to him, and whenever he could manage to get a free seat in the gallery for Shakespeare, Andrew was there. The plays fascinated him, and he learned whole passages from them by heart: all his life afterwards he was able to quote whole scenes. He not only heard the plays, but he read them, for at this time a new influence came into his life, which was to shape the course of many of his actions later on.

53

Colonel Anderson, an Allegheny citizen, was troubled at the fact that few working boys had the money or the opportunity to buy books. He had a small library of his own and he was willing to share his books with boys who were keen to read. He put a notice in the *Pittsburgh Dispatch* that any boy could visit his home on Saturday afternoon and could borrow a book for a week. If the boy proved to be a careful borrower, he could take out a book every week. Andrew Carnegie wasted no time in visiting Colonel Anderson. Week after week he revelled in this new delight of reading. Though he rose at six o'clock each morning and went to work till six o'clock each evening, he spent his evenings with a book. Shakespeare's plays, the essays of Macaulay and Charles Lamb, Plutarch's *Lives,* and volumes of American history became his constant companions. No boy could have made greater use of Colonel Anderson's generosity. Then suddenly a difficulty arose that threatened to stop Andrew's supply of books.

The great success of Colonel Anderson's scheme encouraged him to extend his library to two thousand books, and he established " The Mechanics' and Apprentices' Library " and gave it to the Allegheny Town Council. The Council placed the collection in a special room with a librarian in charge of it, and announced that the library would be free to apprentices, but other boys would have to pay two dollars a year subscription.

Andrew simply could not afford to pay two dollars a year, not if he was to help his mother to pay their debt of twenty pounds to Mrs. Henderson, and this was always foremost in their minds. Andrew went at once to see the librarian.

" What exactly do you mean by an apprentice? " he asked.

" A boy who is bound to a master for a certain number of years to learn a trade," was the librarian's answer.

" But wouldn't a telegraph boy be a kind of apprentice ? "

The librarian shook his head. " No, my lad. You haven't signed any agreement to be bound to your master for a number of years, have you ? "

" No," Andrew admitted.

" Then you are not, strictly speaking, an apprentice."

" Does that mean I can't borrow books from the library ? "

" Not unless you pay the two dollars first."

Two dollars ! That was almost a week's wages ! Andrew knew that he could not ask his mother to pay that for him, great as was his joy in books. Though he left the field of battle, he was not defeated.

" I'll write to the *Pittsburgh Dispatch* about it," he decided, and then and there he wrote his first letter to a newspaper. In it he stated :

> You will remember that Mr. Anderson established and supported a library for working boys and apprentices. Every working boy has been freely admitted, only requiring his parent or guardian to become surety. But its means of doing good have recently been greatly circumscribed by new directors who refuse to allow any boy who is not learning a trade, and bound for a certain time, to become a member. I rather think the new directors have mistaken the generous donor's intentions.

To this the librarian in his turn replied by a letter in the same newspaper. In it he said the free use of the library was intended for apprentices alone. Still Andrew was not beaten ! He wrote yet another letter to the paper, and hammered away at the point that the new regulations were far from Colonel Anderson's intentions. This time he wrote :

> The question is, was the donation intended for the use of apprentices only in the strict meaning of the word, persons learning a trade *and bound,* or whether it was designed for working boys whether bound or not. If the former be

correct, then the managers have certainly misunderstood the generous donor's intentions.

He signed both these letters, " A Working Boy, though not bound."

Three days later a short notice appeared in the newspaper. " ' A Working Boy ' would confer a favour by calling at our office."

Andrew turned up at once at the editor's office and found the librarian there. Together, with the editor's help, they straightened out their differences of opinion, and the librarian consented to stretch the rules to admit " working boys, though not bound."

It was a victory to Andrew indeed, won by his own powers of the pen, but the fruits of victory were sweeter still—the right to borrow books from the apprentices' library. Andrew himself said, " The windows were opened through which the light of knowledge streamed." From that time on, he was never without a book to study.

It was from this boyhood experience that the wish grew in him that all men and women might have the opportunity to borrow books freely; that the wealth of literature might be shared by all. All his life he never forgot his boyhood hunger for books, and it was his secret determination that, if he ever had the means, he would copy Colonel Anderson and give libraries, so that every child, however poor, should be able to borrow books.

Not all his time was spent in reading. There was always the river at their door in Allegheny. Andrew learned to swim himself and he taught his young brother too. Later on, the first gift he ever made to Dunfermline was a swimming bath, perhaps because he had loved this sport so much in his youth. All Andrew Carnegie's great gifts to mankind had something to do with his own youthful experiences and needs.

In winter sometimes the river was frozen and Andrew and his Scottish friends skated upon it. Even when the river was in flood, the boys enjoyed it! Andrew wrote on one occasion to Dod in Dunfermline:

We have had a flood this year. Every season when the snow melts on the mountains, the rivers rise very high, but they have not been so high for twenty years before. It rained for three weeks almost constantly, and both rivers rose at once. It was up to the ceiling in our house, and for two days we had to live upstairs, and sail about in rafts and skiffs. It was a great time.

Mrs. Carnegie would hardly consider it " a great time," and she must have been sorely vexed to see her clean kitchen submerged in a muddy stream. For the boys, however, there was all the fun of novelty in going about in a boat.

Andrew was also a member of the choir at the Swedenborgian Church. Though he had not a great voice, he enjoyed the choral singing and rarely missed a practice. He loved to hear Mr. Koethen, the organist, playing music by Bach and Handel. In later years, when he became rich, he made many gifts of organs to churches. Andrew believed in self-help, and if a congregation would raise half the money required for an organ, Andrew would give them the other half.

In the telegraph office he did his work willingly and well and he showed such common-sense that Mr. Glass, the manager of the downstairs office that dealt with the public, often chose Andrew to look after the office if he was likely to be away from it for half an hour or so. During the time Mr. Glass was away Andrew had to receive messages from people and send them upstairs to be telegraphed. The messages that came from the operating room had also to be sent out, and it was Andrew's duty to send the other boys to deliver them. One Saturday night, when Mr. Glass was paying the boys their monthly wages, Andrew came up to the counter with the others. He was usually the first in the line to be paid. To his surprise Mr. Glass pushed the eleven-and-a-quarter dollars past him to Robert Pitcairn.

"You wait to the last, Andrew. I want to speak to you," Mr. Glass said.

Andrew's heart sank within him and he went very red. He wondered whether he had made some bad mistake and he was going to be given his notice to leave. When the other boys had been paid, Mr. Glass said, "Now, Andrew, just come into my office."

Andrew followed him, feeling very nervous. "Mr. Glass, sir, have I done something wrong?" he stammered. "If I've made a mistake, please give me another chance. I couldn't bear the disgrace——"

"What disgrace?" Mr. Glass asked, mystified.

"The disgrace of losing my job, sir."

Mr. Glass laughed heartily. "Bless the lad! Who said you were going to lose your job? No, no, Andy, I've decided to promote you."

"Promote me, Mr. Glass?" Andrew's head swam.

"Yes, I've decided you're worth more than the other lads. I like the way you've looked after the office when I've had to be out. In future you'll get thirteen-and-a-half dollars a month. That's a rise of two dollars and a quarter."

"Oh, Mr. Glass, I can hardly believe it. Thank you, sir. My mother will be so glad." Still stammering his thanks, Andrew dashed out of the door and scarcely stopped running till he got home. All the way his mind was full of rosy plans for the future.

First of all he handed over his usual wages to his mother; then he waited till all the family were sitting round the table, and with an air of triumph produced the extra money.

"What's this, Andrew?" Mrs. Carnegie cried.

"My extra wages, Mother! I've had a rise. Mr. Glass said he gave it to me because he's pleased with the way I worked."

"Did the other lads get a rise too?" William Carnegie inquired.

" No, Father. Just me."

Mrs. Carnegie had tears of pride in her eyes, and William clapped Andrew on the shoulder. " Well done, laddie ! "

" You wait, Mother ! " Andrew said. " I'll earn enough yet, you'll see, to do what I promised; to let you ride in your own carriage, and it shan't just be in America either, but in Dunfermline for all the folk to see you."

" I almost believe you, Andy," his mother smiled. " My ! This is a great day for the Carnegies. But there's something I must do before I go dreaming of riding in a carriage. Give me yon stocking from underneath the mattress on the bed."

Andrew lifted it out. To his surprise it was quite heavy. Mrs. Carnegie emptied it out on to the table and a small hoard of silver coins came pouring out.

" Mercy me, Margaret ! How did you manage to save those ? " William exclaimed.

" Oh, a silver half-dollar here and another there, scraped together over a long time," Mrs. Carnegie told him. " Andrew's wages have helped, and you've helped me too, William, by going short of many a thing and not grumbling. I got a little extra from the shoe-binding too. It's taken a long time to gather it, bit by bit, but your two dollars will put the finish to it, I'm thinking, Andrew. There should be over eighty dollars there."

" Eighty dollars ! Why, that's twenty pounds ! " Andrew exclaimed. " Whatever will you do with eighty dollars, Mother ? " But even as he asked the question, he knew the answer.

" I can pay back my good friend Ailie Henderson the twenty pounds she lent us to pay our fares to America. She trusted us with her life-savings. There's a friend for you ! I'll never have another like her. I've been saving—saving —I couldn't rest till I'd paid her back." Mrs. Carnegie was near to tears. She controlled herself and said quietly, " On Monday, William, you shall get a draft at the bank and send it off to Dunfermline at once. I can hold my head up now. This is a proud day; my son promoted, and the Carnegies free of debt! "

No success that came to Andrew in after life thrilled him with quite such joy as this one did, his first promotion. He was not long to remain an ordinary telegraph boy. He began to learn the Morse Code so that he could understand the workings of the telegraph key. It was the duty of the telegraph boys to arrive first at the office in the morning to sweep and dust. Their work finished, sometimes the boys had a chance of trying their morse on the telegraph instruments before the operators arrived. Andrew tried to arrive early at the office so that he could play at sending messages with the telegraph key to other telegraph boys in other cities, for their were several boys who were ambitious to become operators.

One morning, when Andrew was alone in the office, the telegraph key began to tap and the Philadelphia call signal began to come through very strongly. Andrew took a chance and answered it. The operator at Philadelphia had an urgent message about a death, and he wanted the message to be delivered in Pittsburgh immediately. He asked if there was anyone in the office at that early hour who could take down a message. Andrew tapped out a halting reply that if the operator would send his message slowly, he would try to take it. So, word by word, Andrew managed to take down the message correctly, and then he ran out at once to deliver it. When he returned, Mr. Brooks was already in the office and wondering why Andrew was not at his desk as usual.

" Hello, Andrew, where have you been till now? " he asked.

" Out with a telegram, Mr. Brooks."

" Out with a telegram! But the office has only just opened. Who took the message from the tapper key? "

" I did, sir," Andrew admitted, wondering whether Mr.

Brooks would be annoyed. " It was a death message from Philadelphia, so I thought it ought to go out at once."

" Oh, and how did you manage to take the message down? "

" I've been teaching myself to use the telegraph instruments, Mr. Brooks."

" The dickens you have ! " Mr. Brooks cried, astonished.

" I'm sorry if I did wrong, Mr. Brooks."

" You were doing your best; there's nothing wrong with that. You must be careful not to make any mistakes, though. Let me see the message. You've kept a copy of it, of course ? "

" Oh, yes, sir ! Here it is." Andrew produced his copy and Mr. Brooks read it through.

" Mm ! Yes, that seems to be in order," he commented. " You've done quite well, Andrew. I'm pleased with the way you've handled this emergency."

Later on, Mr. Brooks told the operator, " Mr. MacLean, whenever you have a few minutes free from operating, perhaps you'll take Andy and give him some instruction. A lad like that is worth teaching. He'll probably make a useful telegraphist some day."

Andrew was soon able to handle the telegraph key with confidence. The messages were printed in morse on a running strip of paper, and then transcribed into ordinary words. Mr. MacLean was a clever operator who could read a message by its sound on the tapper; Andrew tried to imitate him and grew equally clever at " hearing " a message in morse.

There was an old gentleman, Mr. Courtney Hughes, who acted as copyist in the office. It was his work to rewrite the morse messages in plain English. One day, as the operator was not there, Andrew started to take a message and asked Mr. Hughes to rewrite it for him from the tape.

" I'll do it for a proper operator and not for a messenger boy," the old man said with dignity.

To his surprise, Andrew stopped the tape running and took a pencil and paper and began taking the message by ear from the tapper key, writing down the words as they came. Courtney Hughes was astonished. He snatched the pad and read the words on it and he knew from what was on the tape that the message was correct.

" I didn't know you could do that, Andrew," he said, and there was admiration in his voice. After that he was always Andrew's friend and quite willing to copy for him.

Shortly afterwards another opportunity came Andrew's way. The operator at Greensburg, a small town thirty miles away, was to have a fortnight's leave of absence, and some-one from Pittsburgh had to take his place. Mr. Brooks was in a difficulty for he had no experienced operator to send. He thought of Andrew Carnegie.

" Andy, how would you like to go to Greensburg for a fortnight as telegraph operator? " he asked.

Andrew's face beamed with delight at the prospect. " Very much, Mr. Brooks," he said.

" Do you think you could cope with the work all right? Greensburg isn't a very big place and there wouldn't be as many messages as at Pittsburgh, but you'd be all alone there."

" I'd manage all right, sir," Andrew told him with confidence.

Whenever Andrew knew he could do a thing, he had great faith in himself. Some people thought he was a bit too cocksure, but Andrew saw no reason for false modesty.

" Very well, then, we'll give you a trial as operator, and while you are at Greensburg your wages will be four dollars a week. In addition, of course, the telegraph company will pay your expenses there. You can go by stage-coach next week."

Andrew was very thrilled at his first journey alone without his parents, as any lad would be. He found his companions in the mail-coach were a Pittsburgh solicitor and his sister, both Scots, and also another Scotsman. They were all very friendly to the bright-faced lad. The thirty-mile trip to Greensburg was almost like a Caledonian Society meeting, for they talked of Scottish heroes like Wallace and Bruce, and even recited Robert Burns' poetry! In a letter Andrew wrote, " I was quite vexed when the journey was over."

Andrew took this journey in 1852. Journeys still had to be made by coach, along roads that were little better than muddy lanes, but as they rattled along Andrew noticed that work had begun on the track for the Pennsylvania Railroad. Deep cuttings and embankments were being made. Little did Andrew know then how much his own future was to be bound up with this railroad, and how some day it was to bring him the foundation of his great wealth.

The little hotel at Greensburg was also something of an experience for him, for he had never stayed at a coaching inn before and he found the food " wonderfully fine."

He took his lonely job very seriously, and often stayed late at night at the telegraph office. One night there was a severe thunderstorm and Andrew had failed to " earth " his instrument. He ventured near the telegraph key and there was a sudden blinding flash which knocked him off his office stool, stunned him, and very nearly ended his career. He took good care in future not to run any more risks like that.

Andrew did so well at Greensburg that when a new operator was wanted at Pittsburgh Mr. Brooks promoted him. He was now sixteen years old, and his new salary was twenty-five dollars a month, or about twenty-five shillings a week. Though that may sound a very small wage to us nowadays, a hundred years ago it was a very good one indeed for such a young lad. Five pounds a month would then buy more than five pounds a week nowadays, and you may be sure Mrs. Carnegie made the money go a long way and managed to save something out of it too. She herself was still adding to the family income by binding shoes. William Carnegie still plodded away at his hand-loom, as unwilling to admit that the day of the hand-loom weaver was over in America as he had been in Dunfermline. He got an occasional order for linen, and sometimes he peddled his table-cloths from door to door, selling one here and there. If it had not been for Margaret Carnegie's moving spirit, her restless energy, her hard work, the Carnegie family would have fared ill indeed in America during the first years of their life there.

To the telegraph office at Pittsburgh came many telegrams for the Pittsburgh newspapers, bringing the latest foreign news. This fell to Andrew to transcribe, and he began to take a tremendous interest in foreign affairs which lasted all his life. This knowledge proved very useful to him at the Debating Club that the young men of Rebecca Street held in Mr. Phipps, the cobbler's shop. Andrew made copies of all the foreign news for the newspapers and for this he was paid an extra five dollars a month. This gave the Carnegies still more " elbow room," and Andrew was able to pay his subscription to the Webster Literary and Debating Society in Pittsburgh. There Andrew learned to speak with self-possession before an audience, and in his later life he was never terrified of speaking in public. He made two rules for himself. " Be at home with your audience " and " Talk *to* them, not *at* them."

Though Andrew's love for Scotland remained as intense as ever, he was fast becoming an American in thought and feeling. He preferred the greater democratic feeling in America to the conditions existing then in Britain. In a letter to Cousin Dod he says :

We have commenced the great work of reform. We have abolished flogging in the navy. Our postage system is far cheaper than your rates. We have done away with imprisonment for debt. Our public lands are settled with enterprising people. Cities spring up as if by magic. Fifty-two steamboats are launched from Pittsburgh every year. Every district has its splendid public school. Our railroads are extending and Britain cannot supply us with iron fast enough to keep us going. The one country is ' Old England,' and the other is ' Young America.' That is where the secret lies.

Andrew was glorying in being a young American in a young and fast-growing America, and he could see all the advantages in his new country, though Dunfermline and Scotland still tugged at his heart-strings.

During his work in the telegraph office Andrew often met Thomas A. Scott, the superintendent of the Pennsylvania Railroad at Pittsburgh. Andrew transacted most of his business for him with the general superintendent at Altoona. One day, one of Mr. Scott's assistants said, " By the way, Andrew, Mr. Scott has taken a great fancy to you. He asked me if I thought you'd like a job with him as his telegraph clerk and operator on the private railway telegraph."

Andrew's eyes glinted suddenly. " What did you tell him ? " he said.

" Oh, I said I didn't think it was possible. I told him you were already a full operator with the telegraph company, and I didn't think you could be persuaded to leave your present job."

Andrew laid a hand on his arm. " Not so fast ! Mr. Scott can have me if he wants me. Please go and tell him so."

This was one of Andrew's snap decisions that was to affect all his future. For a time he had been feeling that promotion in the telegraph office would only come very slowly. The highest position he was likely to get was manager of a city telegraph office. That was not enough for Andrew. He had been looking round for some time for another post that would give him more opportunities to get on. He had watched the Pennsylvania Railroad being built, and realized what scope it offered for hard-working young men in its organization. He admired Mr. Scott very much as a clever administrator, so when the chance came to work alongside him, Andrew took it at once.

Mr. Scott offered him thirty-five dollars a month to work with him. At the same time Mr. Brooks would have liked to have kept Andrew's services.

" If you will stay with the telegraph company, I'll give you four hundred dollars a year, Andy," he offered.

Andy shook his head. " I'm sorry, Mr. Brooks, but that is twenty dollars a year less than Mr. Scott has offered me. Besides, I honestly think there'll be more chances to get on in the railroad company than in the telegraph office."

" Aye, and ' getting on ' means a great deal to you, doesn't it, Andy? " Mr. Brooks said shrewdly. " Well, you're young and I can't blame you for taking all the chances that come your way."

"Thank you, Mr. Brooks, and I'd like to say how grateful I am to you for all you've done for me during the past five years," Andrew said sincerely, genuinely sorry at parting. But his mind was made up, and he would not change it. Andrew Carnegie could not bear to stand still. There was always the urge in him to make new progress, and that urge he inherited from his mother.

CHAPTER 4

Railway Adventures

In 1853 THERE WERE VERY FEW RAILWAYS IN AMERICA. The Pennsylvania Railroad was a single track from Philadelphia to Pittsburgh. Thomas Scott was a brilliant young man, one of the pioneers in developing communications and transport in the State of Pennsylvania: at the time he took over the management of the railway there had been a number of terrible accidents because both goods and passenger trains were run in opposite directions on the single track. There was no sure method of signalling between station and station. Mr. Scott determined to put an end to the accidents by running a telegraph wire along the track, to send messages about the movements of trains from station to station. It was to work this telegraph that he took Andrew into employment. He had other far-seeing plans for developing the railway: a double track from Philadelphia, a continuous route to the Ohio river, and the building of a line across the mountains.

At first, as his time would not be fully taken up with telegraph work, Andrew was to act as a kind of secretary and right-hand man to Thomas Scott, and share his office. This suited Andrew well enough, for he was devoted to Mr. Scott and admired his energy and powers of organization tremendously. Before very long he was known as " Scott's Andy " all up and down the railroad.

Thomas Scott soon found that Andrew was capable and trustworthy. One of Andrew's duties was to go to Altoona, the headquarters of the railway, to get the monthly pay packets and cheques for the Pittsburgh division. Andrew, of course, travelled by train. Some parts of the old tracks were very rough indeed, but Andrew scorned the luxury of a compartment. He much preferred riding on the engine with the driver and fireman, for he was friendly with many of them.

On one particular day he started out with the pay packet and cheques tucked under his waistcoat for safety, as they were too big to go into his pocket. As usual he rode on the footplate of the engine. This time the engine rode very roughly over a bad piece of track, and Andrew, jolted and shaken around on the footplate, had to hold tight with both hands. Suddenly he felt for the pay packet under his waistcoat. It had gone!

" Stop! " he cried to the engine driver. " Stop, man! I've lost the pay packet! "

" What? " shouted the driver above the rattle of the train.

" The pay packet! It's gone! It must have been shaken out of my clothes and dropped off the engine." Andrew was white-faced : the precious pay packet! Mr. Scott would never trust him again. " Stop the engine! I've got to go back! "

The driver slowed down to a crawl. " Are you sure you had it when you got on the train? "

" Sure! Positive! It was up my waistcoat only a minute or two ago. I had it then, I know I had! It must have fallen on to the track. Stop the train, I've got to find it! "

" There's a quicker way than that. I'll reverse the engine and run back slowly for a couple of miles," the good-natured driver said, sorry for Andrew's distress. " You watch the track, youngster."

It was a lucky thing that trains were not very frequent in this stretch of the railway, for in a few moments the astonished passengers found they were going backwards! Andrew watched the track anxiously. Suddenly he cried, " Stop! It's there! "

On the bank of a large stream, only a foot or two from the water's edge, lay the precious package! Andrew nipped down from the footplate like lightning and caught it up. He examined it carefully. Nothing was missing. Then with a long sigh of relief he climbed aboard again, and thanked the driver heartily.

" Aye, but take better care of it, Andy, or you might not be so lucky next time," the engine driver told him. " Suppose it had fallen in the stream and been swept away? Ah, well, we'll get up steam again and make up time."

" I'm sorry for delaying you."

" Don't worry, we'll get to Pittsburgh punctually, you'll see. Jim'll put an extra shovelful of coal on the fire now and again, eh, Jim? " John winked at the fireman. " What's more," he added seriously, " we'll not tell a word of this to anyone, for we don't want you to get into trouble, Andy."

The two men kept their promise and no one else got to know of Andrew's mishap. From then on, he always held on tightly to the pay packet and never let it out of his grasp. It was years afterwards that he told what had happened, and then he said, " Since then I have never believed in being too hard on a young man if he makes a mistake or two," for he realized what a difference the total loss of that package might have made to his own career.

This was a far rougher life than Andrew had led in the telegraph office, but it toughened him both in body and spirit. In the hard weather he wore loosely-fitting garments tucked into heavy boots, and a huge winter coat over all, for much of his work for Mr. Scott took him to the railway construction camps. He rode in the cabs of railway engines and even slept on the floors of freight trains. He mixed with the tough railway gangs and grew to like them, in spite of their rough ways, as they grew to like him. It was at this time that he learned how to control workmen and to speak with authority, even though it was really Mr. Scott's authority behind him. This training was to be very useful later on, and Andrew's confidence in himself, never lacking, grew still more.

Andrew believed in himself and his own powers so much that, from time to time, he would risk all his own future on his own judgment. He eagerly undertook responsibility far beyond his own years. One day he arrived at the office to find Mr. Scott was not there and the assistant telegraphist was looking very worried indeed.

" Hullo ! What's wrong, Davy ? " Andrew asked as he took off his coat.

" I'm glad you've come, Andy. There's been a bad accident in the Eastern Division," his assistant told him. " It has delayed the west-bound express. There's an east-bound passenger train in the same section and it's just crawling along with a man holding a red flag walking in front of it at every curve."

" Where's Mr. Scott ? "

" He hasn't come in yet, I sent to his house but he's not there."

Andrew rubbed his chin and considered what to do.

" What about the other trains—the freight trains ? " he asked. " What's happened to them ? "

" They've been standing in the sidings all up and down the line for most of the night."

" Sakes alive ! The poor chaps in them must be wearied out and half-frozen lying out there all night in this bitter weather. I'll have to do something about it, Davy."

" But what *can* you do, Andy ? " Davy protested. " You know that Mr. Scott is the only person who gives orders to move trains."

" I believe I could set things in motion all right," Andrew said with confidence, " I always telegraph Mr. Scott's orders

70

In a few minutes the telegraph boy was tapping briskly

for him, and I know just what he'd do in an emergency like this. I've *got* to get those trains moving again, Davy. I can send the orders in Mr. Scott's name."

Davy looked shocked, for this seemed rather too bold a plan for him, but Andrew was paying him no attention but was staring at a railway map on the wall and moving pins about on it that represented the various trains.

" Let's see——" he thought aloud : " The east-bound passenger train can move to Johnstown and stand in the siding there till the west-bound freight train for Wheeling has moved out of the way——"

In a few minutes the telegraph key was tapping briskly and Andrew was moving trains up and down the line and restoring order out of chaos just as he knew Mr. Scott would have done. He boldly signed all the telegraph messages " Thomas A. Scott." It was a very great risk to take, and any mishap would have brought Andrew's railroad career to an immediate end : cocksure he may have been, but he certainly had the sense and ability to handle an emergency. For over an hour Andrew Carnegie sat at the telegraph key and sent out instructions. From station to station he took the trains, checking every movement and taking every precaution to avoid another accident. Just as he had got all the trains running smoothly again Mr. Scott dashed into the office.

" Well, Andrew, there's trouble, I hear. How are matters? " he asked and, expecting a report of delays from Andrew, he took pencil and writing pad. " We must get these trains started at once. Send off these orders as we go along, Andy."

Andrew, realizing for the first time what a risky thing he had done, looked worried.

" Mr. Scott, I couldn't find you anywhere, so I gave these orders in your name early this morning," and he handed Mr. Scott the copies of the telegraph messages he had sent.

Mr. Scott was considerably startled. "*You* gave orders, Andy?"

"In your name, sir."

Mr. Scott shuffled quickly through the sheaf of telegrams. "Well, are the trains going all right? Where is the Eastern Express?"

"Here, sir, at this point. She's proceeding east very slowly. Those are the messages and the latest reports from the stations. This freight train here has reached Harrisburg all right. There's another freight train standing in this siding waiting to be moved next, Mr. Scott. I can give you the position of every train on the line."

Mr. Scott looked Andrew straight in the face. Though his expression was one of reproof, it was also one of admiration. Andrew dared scarcely meet his eyes.

"Mm! You seem to have got the railway working again, my lad. Well, if it comes out all right—that's all right. Now just go over these messages with me again." He spoke no word of blame, but Andrew understood that he had taken a tremendous responsibility and that he had been lucky as well as clever.

Andrew felt a little distressed lest what he had done should have offended Mr. Scott, always his friend and hero, but later on he heard from Mr. Franciscus, the head of the freight department, that Mr. Scott had said to him, "Do you know what that little fair-haired Scotch rascal of mine did?"

"No?"

"I'm blamed if he didn't run every train in the division in my name, without my authority."

"And did he do it all right?"

"Oh, yes, everything was all right," Mr. Scott admitted.

For a lad not yet twenty years old to have run a whole railway by himself was something of an achievement. What he had done was even brought to the notice of the President of

73

the Pennsylvania Railroad, John Edgar Thomson. From then on Mr. Scott gave more and more responsibility to Andrew Carnegie, and Andrew was looked upon as showing great promise as a future railway official. When Mr. Scott had again to be absent from his office he put Andrew in charge of it, and he raised Andrew's wages to forty dollars a month. America was indeed proving a land of opportunity for Andrew and realizing Mrs. Carnegie's dream.

The Carnegies were indeed beginning to find their feet in the New World. Not only was their debt to Mrs. Henderson paid, but Mrs. Carnegie was steadily saving money and Andrew's good wages were providing various small comforts in the home, a bureau and a rocking chair for Mrs. Carnegie among other things. Uncle and Aunt Hogan had also been prospering and had removed to a new house in another part of the town. The Carnegies held a family council and decided to buy the Hogans' house and ground. Mr. and Mrs. Hogan allowed them two years to pay for the house, paying part of the debt with interest every half-year. From then on every dollar was saved to pay off the amount still due on the house.

In 1855, when the debt was almost cleared off, Andrew's father died. Andrew was then not quite twenty years old. He had to take on the responsibility for the whole household and the management of their money affairs, though he was better able to cope with business matters than William Carnegie had been. Sad as they all were to lose their kind father, hard work left them no time to mope. Andrew's brother Tom was still at school, and Mrs. Carnegie kept on with her work of binding shoes to help Andrew's wages. By very careful planning and making every economy, they managed to pay the funeral expenses and the debt as well. The Carnegies now owned their own house.

But shortly afterwards, Mr. Scott and Andrew had a momentous conversation.

" Andrew, if you have five hundred dollars saved, I have an investment I could recommend to you," Mr. Scott said.

Although five hundred cents (halfpence) was nearer what Andrew had in the bank at the time, he asked, " What company should I invest in, sir? "

" The Adams Express Company. It's a very good company indeed and it will make big profits, you'll see. I think it would pay you if you could afford the money for the shares."

" May I think it over this evening and have a talk with my mother first? "

" Oh, yes, by all means," Mr. Scott replied.

When Andrew got home that evening he told his mother about Mr. Scott's suggestion. " I wish we had enough money to buy the shares, Mother, for I am sure Mr. Scott would never have recommended them to me if he didn't know they were good."

Margaret Carnegie had the same boldness of decision that Andrew had. She never failed to see, either, what might be for the good of her children. She asked one or two questions and then she said, " There's the house. That is worth five hundred dollars and it is our own now."

" But we shouldn't want to sell our home."

" No, but we might raise a loan on it. Perhaps we can borrow the money and repay a certain sum each half-year, and give the house-papers as a pledge that we will pay. Mortgage it, in fact."

" But if we failed to pay the money at the right time— then the person who lent it might take the house."

" Yes, but it is worth taking the risk. I shall not do the business through a stranger. I'll consult your uncle William Morrison first. I think he would lend us the money. I'll go by steamer to his farm first thing to-morrow. You can tell Mr. Scott that you can arrange to buy the shares."

William Morrison was doing very well as a farmer in the

Ohio valley. Mrs. Carnegie returned the same day with the five hundred dollars in her pocket. She had never failed Andrew when he needed her help. He took the money in triumph to Mr. Scott next day, and the shares became his.

Andrew now had another object in life—to pay off the five hundred dollars for which his mother had mortgaged their home. The Adams Express Company proved a very good thing indeed. Every month Andrew received a cheque from the company for ten dollars. This was always set aside with other savings towards paying off their debt. It was not long before the debt was paid and Andrew and his mother owned both the house and the shares in the Adams Express Company too. Andrew had found a way to make his money work for him!

At this time, too, Andrew was seized with a new ambition. He had written a letter to a Pittsburgh newspaper about the Pennsylvania Railroad, and this had attracted the notice of Mr. Stokes, the chief lawyer for the railway. He became interested in Andrew and his intelligent grasp of affairs and he invited Andrew to visit him at his house. Mr. Stokes had a very fine house indeed, but what impressed Andrew most was that Mr. Stokes had one room full of books, his library. On the mantelpiece was carved an open book with an inscription :

> He that cannot reason is a fool.
> He that will not is a bigot.
> He that dare not is a slave.

" Some day I shall have a library of my own like this one," Andrew vowed to himself. " And I will have those words carved upon my mantelpiece too."

Mr. Scott was promoted to be the General Superintendent of the Pennsylvania Railroad in 1856. Andrew Carnegie was then twenty-two years old, and Mr. Scott asked him to go with him to the railway headquarters at Altoona. This meant Andrew leaving his home in Allegheny and going into lodgings at Altoona's railway hotel. Although it meant a split for a time in their home life and his mother missed him very much, she would never have dreamed of standing in Andrew's way to promotion. His advancement in life was of more importance to her than any other thing.

Unfortunately, as soon as Mr. Scott took up his new appointment, a railway strike was threatened. One night there was a knock at Andrew's door. It was a messenger from the telegraph office at Altoona.

" Andrew, a message has just come in and the strike situation is getting worse. The freight train men have left their train at Miflin and they refuse to move it. The line's blocked and all traffic's stopped. Something must be done at once."

Andrew hesitated. Mr. Scott had been out on the railways till very late the previous night and, dog-tired, he was now fast asleep.

" I hardly like to wake Mr. Scott and get him up again. He's been so overworked lately," Andrew said, but this was something that Mr. Scott really ought to know. Andrew went to him, woke him and explained the situation quickly. Mr. Scott groaned sleepily.

" Maybe I could deal with it, sir? " Andrew suggested with his usual confidence. " I'll telegraph to some of the leaders and suggest they come to see you to-morrow at Altoona."

" Very well," Mr. Scott agreed, so Andrew went back to the telegraph offices and messages were flashed back and forth between Altoona and Miflin, from Andrew to the strike leaders. Andrew's great powers of persuasion succeeded with the men and they consented to go back to work and move the train, on the condition that Mr. Scott would give them a hearing in Altoona next day. Once more Andrew was successful in getting the railroad traffic on the move.

As well as being dependable and clever at his work, Andrew was certainly lucky. One day, when he was travelling on business for the railway company to a town in Ohio, he sat in the rear compartment on the end seat, dreamily watching the track fall away behind the train. Just then a tall thin man, in appearance very like a farmer, approached him.

" The brakesman told me you were an official of the Pennsylvania Railroad, sir. May I have the pleasure of a word with you? "

The stranger had such a dignified convincing manner that Andrew immediately made room for him on the seat beside him.

" My name is Theodore Woodruff. I have something here I would like to show you." The man opened a small carpet bag and produced a queer-looking model from it. Andrew looked at it with curiosity.

" It is a sleeping car for use on the railways," Mr. Woodruff explained. " I have just got the patent rights for it."

Anything to do with railways had a tremendous interest for Andrew. He turned the little model carefully over in his hands while Woodruff explained it.

" It is really a seat-and-coach car," he said. " You see, in the day-time the bed folds up to make two ordinary seats facing each other, as in a compartment now. At night-time, a board can be pulled out from underneath and the seats converted into a bed."

" Yes, but what about the bedclothes? " Andrew asked.

" Here is a second bed that can be let down by chains and hinges from the ceiling of the compartment. All the blankets for both beds can be stored in this one during the day-time, and it can be pulled up to the ceiling out of the way."

Andrew's eyes danced with excitement as he examined

the model, and changed the seats into a bed and back again. It fascinated him. He had never seen anything like it before. He knew that, as the great railways of America extended westward, some really comfortable sleeping accommodation would have to be provided, for people might have to spend several days and nights in a train. Mr. Woodruff's little model seemed to be the answer to this.

Up till now the only kind of sleeping car the railroad had was a freight car with wooden bunks built along its sides. Only men passengers slept in these, stretched out on the uncomfortable wooden beds, with their overcoats thrown over them. No woman would have dreamed of travelling in them, for there was no privacy and the bunks were often extremely dirty. It was more comfortable to travel sitting upright in a compartment. The new design gave comfort and privacy too, as well as an economical way of providing seating accommodation and sleeping car together.

Andrew knew that the railways were just beginning their big building programmes : little by little the stage-coach and the covered wagon would vanish altogether, and trains would take their places. He looked at Woodruff's model with more and more enthusiasm as its importance grew upon him. Again he made one of his quick decisions.

" Yes, this is certainly something we must have on the Pennsylvania Railroad," he told Woodruff. " I would like Mr. Scott, the railway superintendent, to see this model. Could you come to Altoona if I sent for you ? "

" I certainly could ! " Woodruff agreed readily, and Andrew made a note of his address.

Andrew was so excited at the possibilities of the model sleeping-car that he was all impatience to get back to Altoona and tell Mr. Scott about Woodruff's model. As soon as he returned he burst into Mr. Scott's office with the great news.

" Mr. Scott ! I've seen something that will solve one of

79

the greatest railway problems of the future ! " he cried. But Mr. Scott took the matter far more calmly than Andrew did.

" That's all right, Andy, but we haven't built the vast railways that are going to need many sleeping cars yet," he pointed out.

Andrew's enthusiasm was not to be dashed at all. " But they're coming, Mr. Scott ! Some day the great railways will extend right across America from the Atlantic to the Pacific ! "

Mr. Scott shared this dream too, but he replied, " You're taking time by the forelock, aren't you, Andy ? It'll be many a long day before all these railways are constructed."

" But we've got to be ready for them, Mr. Scott," Andrew persisted. " The day will come when we're going to need sleeping cars badly. We could use some of them now on our long distance trains, and I am sure people would pay extra to sleep in comfort. If we don't take them up, Mr. Woodruff will just sell this idea to some other railway company."

This argument carried some weight with Mr. Scott, for all the railways were in fierce competition with each other then, and these were days of great railways building. Besides that, Mr. Scott had a great opinion of Andrew's foresight. He smiled at him indulgently.

" You are enthusiastic, young man. All the same, you can telegraph for Mr. Woodruff and ask him to come and see me."

Theodore Woodruff came and brought his model sleeping-car with him, and Mr. Scott was as impressed with it as Andrew had been. The result of the interview was that the Pennsylvania Railroad offered to buy two of Mr. Woodruff's sleeping cars as soon as they could be built.

Mr. Woodruff formed a company to build his sleeping cars, and to Andrew's surprise he offered him one-eighth of the shares in his business in gratitude for what Andrew had done for him. This does not mean that he made Andrew a present of the shares in his company, but that he allowed Andrew to buy one-eighth of his whole business. The first payment Andrew would have to make would be about two hundred dollars. Andrew decided he would find the money somehow and he went to see his bank manager, Mr. Lloyd.

Besides putting money into a bank, people can also borrow from a bank. Many folk do not realize that banks will lend money, but they usually require security for doing it. Security can be provided in various ways : by allowing the bank to hold papers ("deeds") concerning property; insurance certificates; certificates of shares in other businesses. These the bank has the right to sell, if the money is not repaid by a certain time. Usually a bank does not sell its customer's property unless there is no chance of the money ever being repaid. Of course, interest has to be paid on any money borrowed from a bank.

Andrew asked Mr. Lloyd if the bank would lend him the money to buy the shares in Woodruff's company. He offered the shares he already possessed in the Adams Express Company as security.

Mr. Lloyd knew Andrew well from his dealings with the Pennsylvania Railroad Company, and he knew in what esteem Andrew was held by the officials. He put his hand on Andrew's shoulder and said at once, " Why, of course, I will lend the money. You are all right, Andrew. I know it's safe enough with you."

Andrew felt very proud of this confidence in him and he signed a note promising to repay the money by a certain date.

Woodruff's sleeping cars were a great success. They were at once in great demand by the passengers on the Pennsylvania Railroad because of the long distances to be travelled. Not only the Pennsylvania Railroad, but several other railways took them up too. Woodruff sold them to the railway companies as fast as he could build them. The interest that

Woodruff paid to Andrew for his one-eighth share was even greater in one year than Andrew had put into the business! By the time Andrew had reached the age of twenty-five, Woodruff's company was paying him five thousand dollars a year, about a thousand pounds in British money. This was the real start of the vast fortune that Andrew Carnegie made later on, for, of course, being a sensible young man, he did not spend all the money he had coming in. He bought shares with it in other companies too that also did very well.

After Andrew had been for a time with Mr. Scott in Altoona, it was decided to remove the Carnegie family to Altoona and to sell the house in Rebecca Street. About one thing Andrew had firmly made up his mind; that his mother was no longer going to be the household drudge. For many long years, in addition to binding shoes, she had cooked, washed and mended for her family. Nothing was too much to do for Andrew and Tom. Andrew was determined that his mother was to have some well-earned rest. The Carnegies would employ a servant-maid!

Mrs. Carnegie did not like the idea at all. She hated the thought of handing over her tasks to someone else who might not do them so well. Andrew's position with the railway, however, required that he should have a bigger house in which to entertain business friends. Slowly he brought his mother round to see the necessity for this. When any change was to be for Andrew's advantage, Margaret Carnegie could never oppose it. She knew that her son was bound to rise in the world of business, and saw that she must be prepared to entertain people for him.

" Dear Mother, you have done everything for Tom and me," Andrew had pleaded. " Now, let me do something for you. Let us be partners and do what is best for each other. The time has come for you to play the lady. One of these days you will ride in your carriage. Meanwhile, get that servant girl in to help you. Tom and I would like that."

At this she gave in and a servant-girl was installed in the Altoona home, but Mrs. Carnegie was far from happy about it at first, and the servant did not have a very easy life! Later on Margaret Carnegie delighted in the extra freedom she had, to have Andrew's friends to the house and to visit them with him.

After Andrew had been nearly three years at Altoona, Mr. Scott was appointed Vice-President of the railway. His new office was to be in Philadelphia. Mr. Scott called Andrew into his private office. " Now, Andy, it has been finally settled that I am to move into Philadelphia. Mr. Enoch Lewis, the Divisional Superintendent, is to take my place here."

" Yes, Mr. Scott." Andrew waited patiently to know what was to become of himself.

" Now," Mr. Scott said briskly. " Do you think you could manage the Pittsburgh Division? "

Andrew was taken by surprise for a moment, but only for a moment! At twenty-four years of age Andrew felt he could manage anything! Nothing daunted him.

" Yes, Mr. Scott, I think I can," he said promptly.

" Well, I have recommended you to the Railway President for the post. He agrees with me that you are worth a trial. Now, there is the question of your new salary and what it is right for you to have."

Andrew cared far more for the position he was to have than for any increase in wages. It was joy enough for him that he was to step into his hero's shoes, for Thomas Scott had once managed the Pittsburgh Division. He did not even wish to bargain about his money but to leave it to Mr. Scott, who he knew would treat him fairly.

" You can make my salary just what you please, Mr. Scott," he said.

" Now, let me see! At present you are getting sixty-five dollars a month," Mr. Scott said. " That is seven hundred and eighty dollars a year. When I managed the Pittsburgh Division I got fifteen hundred dollars a year. The next man got eighteen hundred dollars."

Andrew waited in silence while Mr. Scott considered the matter.

" I think it is only right to double your present money, Andrew, as you will have double the responsibility now. I shall start you at fifteen hundred dollars and if you do well you shall be raised to eighteen hundred dollars."

Andrew was more than delighted, as any young man would be who had suddenly had his wages doubled. What was more, he was now a very responsible official of the railway, and he would now sign his own orders in his own name.

The promotion meant another removal for the Carnegies, this time back to Pittsburgh, where they already had many friends. Another advantage was that Tom, who had followed Andrew's footsteps and become a telegraphist, was to join the railway company as Andrew's secretary, so Andrew made a good opening for his brother too.

The Carnegies rented a house in Eighth Street, but Mrs. Carnegie found Pittsburgh a very dirty place after Altoona. Pittsburgh was developing as a centre of heavy industry. Big chimneys poured out their smoke day and night, smoke that seemed to penetrate everywhere and leave a layer of soot behind.

" Look at these curtains ! " Mrs. Carnegie would grumble. " It's less than a week since they were put up clean and now they look like dusters. Touch the stair bannister and your hands come away black ! If you wash your hands and face they're dirty again in an hour. As for washing clothes, it's a waste of good work ! They come in from the line smothered in soot ! "

She was so miserable at the grime and soot with which she could not keep pace that Andrew decided the only thing was to move to the country.

" Mother will never settle in Pittsburgh. She can't keep the house clean ! " he confided in David Stewart, Mr. Scott's nephew. " I wish I could find some nice little place in the country near enough for me to journey in and out of Pittsburgh every day."

" Why don't you come and live beside us at Homewood ? " David Stewart suggested. " There's a house for sale right next door to us."

Homewood was just a small village inhabited by about a dozen families. Every house had a lovely garden about it. Andrew decided to buy the house his friend recommended and in a short time the Carnegies were settled in Homewood.

Margaret Carnegie was happy and delighted in the new home. All her life she had had a dream too : it was not like Andrew's dream, to ride in her own carriage, but a dream of having a lovely flower garden and of keeping chickens. Now Andrew had made her dream come true. Around the garden were pleasant green woods and a little running stream, and in that sunny place Margaret Carnegie grew masses of flowers. Never had her life been so happy !

They were mostly well-to-do families that lived at Homewood, with many young people. This small community welcomed the Carnegies, and soon they were being invited to parties and musical evenings and giving parties in return. Andrew was beginning to live in a world that was far removed from the poor cottage in Dunfermline or the frame house in Rebecca Street, though he never looked down on his humble beginnings, but was proud of them. Dunfermline and Rebecca Street always held a place in his heart. Part of Andrew's charm was that he never pretended to be anyone but himself, and he was never ashamed of being the son of a hand-loom weaver.

Andrew had a great gift of fun that made him very popular with everyone he met. The quick jokes, the mischievous laugh, together with his small size, made him almost puckish at times. In the country he loved to wear country clothes, which included rather clumsy shoes.

" What big feet you've got, Andrew Carnegie ! " one of the girls at a party exclaimed. " Just look at the size of your shoes ! "

Andrew was always ready with a reply. " Big feet indeed ! I guess I could wear *your* shoes ! "

" I don't believe it, but we'll see," the girl laughed, and she ran off to get one of her daintiest shoes for Andrew to try on.

" I feel a bit like Cinderella ! " Andrew said as he took his own shoe off.

" You mean one of the Ugly Sisters ! " but her laughter turned to surprise when Andrew easily slipped his foot inside her shoe !

" Girls ! Look ! " she cried. " He's actually succeeded in putting on my shoe ! "

" Succeeded ! Why, my foot wobbles about inside it ! "

The days in Homewood were happy ones indeed; skating in winter at which Andrew was very expert; walking, riding on horseback, dancing all filled his spare time. These pursuits balanced his hard work as superintendent of a railway division and gave him a chance to cultivate another side of his nature, the side that loved books and music, gaiety and friends. Andrew began to be more careful of his speech; to be gentle in manner to his friends; to read even more extensively, and to be polite and considerate, as the other young people were who lived in Homewood. These happy days lasted till the outbreak of the Civil War in America in 1861.

CHAPTER 5

Civil War in America

FOR SOME TIME CLOUDS OF WAR HAD BEEN GATHERING IN the United States. The Northern States and the Southern States could not agree on the question of slavery. People like the Carnegies had settled in the north, people who tilled their own ground and worked in factories. In the north there were no slaves. It was quite different in the Southern States like Virginia, Carolina, Georgia, and Alabama. It was to these states that for two hundred years the cruel slave traders had been bringing the negroes they captured in Africa. They brought them, chained together, men, women and children, in the holds of ships. The slaves often had no room to lie down properly to sleep and they were given very little food and water on these terrible voyages.

When they arrived they were sold in the market places like cattle, to land-owners who bought them to labour on the cotton and tobacco plantations. All the labour in the fields was done by negroes and most of the house servants were negroes too. Some of them were treated well, but many of those who worked on the land were driven by whips, and they were all slaves, working without wages, for what food and clothing their owners cared to give them.

A slave had no rights at all. There was no law to protect him. His master had the right to flog him. It was a crime to teach a negro to read or to let him learn a trade. This was the darkest side of slavery. Of course there were many kind masters, and household slaves were often looked on with great affection by the families they served. For all that, they were slaves, and could be sold in the market-place if their owner died. Families of slaves could be parted from each other, husbands from wives and children from their parents.

In 1850 the cotton plantations of the south were doing very well indeed. There was a growing demand for raw cotton from Lancashire where the cotton mills were growing in number. The planters in the Southern States wanted more and more slaves to till their lands. Many planters gained great wealth from the labour of their slaves. In the Northern States, however, there was a growing feeling that slavery was wicked and wrong, and that a country which was called " the land of the free " should have no slaves.

At this time settlers were continually moving westwards and new lands were being brought into cultivation and new towns built. New states were created which wished to join the Union. The Northern States tried to make laws which would prevent slave labour in these new states. The Southern States opposed the making of these laws, and demanded that for every free state without slaves, a slave state should be included in the Union.

Trouble began to come to a head in 1855 when the State of Kansas was being settled. Should it be a slave state or a a free state? Men from the north and south poured in to seize the lands of Kansas. Those from the south made laws in favour of slavery: those from the north were ready to fight for freedom. There were many small pitched battles between the northern and the southern settlers, but in the end the party for freedom won the day and Kansas became a free state.

It was at this time that John Brown led a raid into Virginia to try to rouse a rebellion among the slaves. He was caught by the southern slave owners, condemned to death, and hanged. His death set the whole country in an uproar. It was about John Brown that the famous song was written :

" John Brown's body lies a-mouldering in the grave,
    But his soul goes marching on."

It was true indeed, for John Brown's death was like a battle-cry to all the forces of freedom. In the north the feeling against slavery grew more strongly than ever.

The Southern States were so angry at the interference of the Northern States in what they considered their own affairs that some of the States decided to come out of the Union and break off with the north altogether. They said they would have their own government and elect their own President.

At the beginning of 1861 a new President of the United States had to be elected. The Northern States supported Abraham Lincoln, a great opponent of slavery. They won, and Lincoln was elected President. This was the signal for the Southern States to break away. The men of the south seized government buildings and hauled down the flag of the stars and stripes. This roused tremendous feeling in the Northern States, for it was felt that no state should be allowed to leave the Union. Matters might have been arranged peaceably, but the folk of the Southern States struck the first blow. They fired on Fort Sumter in Carolina, manned by a United States garrison, and they seized the fort. The thought that the flag of the United States had been fired upon roused the Northern States to action. President Lincoln called for an army of 75,000 men and twice that number came forward as volunteers. War between North and South was declared.

Andrew heard the news that the Southerners, who were called the Confederates, had taken Fort Sumter as he went in a crowded train to his office in Pittsburgh. The train hummed like a beehive with the news. " They have fired on the flag ! Fired on our flag ! " was heard on every hand. Andrew said, " Men could not sit still or control their feelings." The news united the Northern States as nothing else could do. The armies formed and everywhere men were drilling and practising with muskets.

Pittsburgh, the head of the iron industry, immediately offered all its men and materials to the service of the north, and among the first to enrol was Andrew Carnegie. Andrew had always called himself a man of peace, and all his life his principles had been against war; but he felt that this was a just war, first to abolish slavery and next to preserve the American Union of States.

The railways of Pennsylvania were of tremendous importance in transporting men and munitions, and Mr. Scott was appointed Assistant Secretary of War in charge of Transport. On his shoulders was the responsibility of organizing railroads and telegraphs. Scott at once asked Andrew to act as his assistant, and, of course, Andrew accepted his invitation.

In April 1861 Abraham Lincoln was at the capital, Washington, and the Confederates were marching on it from the south. They had destroyed part of the railway line between Baltimore and Washington, cutting off the capital from the northern armies that were rushing to defend the city. The situation was full of danger. If Washington were taken by the Confederates and President Lincoln captured, a terrible blow would be dealt to the forces of the north. Abraham Lincoln paced up and down the floor of the White House in Washington, saying, " Why don't they come? Why don't they come? " for he had been told that northern troops were on their way to save the city. He could not understand the delay.

To Scott and his assistant, Andrew Carnegie, fell the task of repairing the railroad so that the northern troops could reach Washington and save the capital and the President.

Andrew collected a force of railway men, train men, track repairers, bridge builders and road makers, and went by an old ferry-boat to Annapolis, from where a branch line

Andrew set his men to work at once

joined the main line to Washington. The Confederates had worked havoc on the lines at Annapolis Junction, and Andrew set his men to work at once to repair this stretch and make it safe for heavy trains. On board the ferry-boat was the Eighth Massachusetts Regiment, and Andrew pressed these willing men into his service. Rails and sleepers were replaced and a bridge rebuilt. In three days Carnegie had the railway track repaired and the troops marched along it while their gear was taken by train. At night they were shot at by men who hid in the woods, but little harm was done.

The first train that travelled over the repaired line to Washington carried Andrew Carnegie in the engine-driver's cab. All the way along he was watching the telegraph wires to see if they had been damaged. At one point he found they had been pinned to the ground by wooden stakes: he stopped the engine and jumped off to release the wires. When Andrew plucked the stakes away, the wires sprang upward, gashing him in the face and knocking him over. So, with blood streaming from a cut, almost like a wounded hero, Andrew entered the city of Washington with the first troops among the cheering crowds. During the next few days General Butler and his army travelled over the repaired line to the relief of Washington. Andrew Carnegie had done a good job of work!

Andrew was given an office in the War Department next to Mr. Scott's, and his first task on arrival was to organize a force of telegraphists. He sent a telegram at once to his old friend David McCargo, who had been his friend in Rebecca Street, and one of the five messenger boys with Andrew in Pittsburgh. David McCargo was also doing well as a railroad superintendent of telegraphs. Andrew's telegram read:

David McCargo, Superintendent of Telegraphists, Pennsylvania Railroad Company, Altoona. Send four of your best operators to Washington at once prepared to enter Government Service for the war. Andrew Carnegie.

David promptly sent four of his best men. This was the start of the telegraph force which later numbered fifteen hundred! The American Civil War marked the beginning of modern war, in which transport and communications are of first importance. It was the military telegraph in Washington that kept Abraham Lincoln in touch with his armies.

It was soon plain that a big attack was coming from the Confederates in the south, with the hope of capturing Washington. In early June Andrew Carnegie went to Alexandria and opened a telegraph station there, as one of the near points where they could expect the attack to begin. Already the Confederates had destroyed many of the railroads, bridges and telegraphs in this area. For more than six weeks Andrew and his repair force worked night and day to make good the damage and to build new lines and tracks.

Andrew was still at Alexandria when the battle of Bull Run was fought on Sunday, July 21, 1861. When the attack came, Andrew was in the telegraph office at Burke's Station, about five miles from the battlefield. His duty was to transmit messages sending troops into battle, and to make arrangements to withdraw the wounded.

The Confederate troops got the upper hand and pressed the attack so hotly that the northern troops were forced to give way. They fell back, then a retreat began which ended in a rout, with northern men running away from the battlefield. Andrew was at Burke's Station when the hordes of retreating men began to descend upon them. He wrote about it:

> I loaded train after train of the poor wounded volunteers. It was soon evident that we must rush every engine and car to the front to bring back our defeated soldiers. The rebels were reported to be close upon us, and we were finally compelled to close Burke's Station. The telegraph operator and I were the last to leave on the train for Alexandria.

At Alexandria the panic was little better, but Andrew

always took pride that every telegraph operator remained at his post and not one of them lost his head and joined the stampeding mob. Every man did his work till the battle was over.

It was feared for a time that the Confederates would follow up their victory and march on Washington, but they stopped short at Alexandria and that gave the northern armies breathing space to re-organize and re-equip their men and restore their shattered lines of communication.

For the Northern States their defeat at Bull Run seemed a crashing disaster at the time, but it had the effect of uniting the north more than ever before, and making the people grimly determined to ensure that no more such victories should be won by the south. Up till now the war had been almost a half-hearted affair. Now that the north knew what they were up against, and that there would be no easy victories for them, they organized wholeheartedly for war. In one of Andrew Carnegie's letters written five days after the defeat at Bull Run he wrote :

Depend upon it, the recent defeat is a blessing in disguise. We shall now begin in earnest. Knowing our foes the necessary means will be applied to ensure their overthrow. What might have been half work, a mere scotching of the snake, will now be thorough and complete, and you shall, at no distant time, be able to proclaim that God has made all men free and equal, and that slavery is the sum of all the villainies.

In this letter he shows his great powers to think ahead and reason what would happen. This is one of the qualities that made him great. He was glad, too, to feel that he was of use in this war for freedom in which he believed so strongly. He went on to say in the same letter :

I am delighted with my occupation here—hard work, but gratifying to lie down at night and think that I am some use in sustaining a great cause and making the truth clearer for those who come hereafter.

94

That was Andrew Carnegie, always optimistic, always confident in the right, even though those around him might be plunged into gloom, always able to see the glimmer of light through the darkness of anxiety, always looking forward.

Andrew said little of himself during the battle of Bull Run, but the truth is that besides being within range of the guns he suffered a sunstroke on that terrible July day. It was extremely hot and the heat caused great misery to everyone, especially the wounded, whom Andrew saw packed into trains in all their suffering, to be taken away from the battlefield. It was a sad and terrible experience for him, but as he boarded that last train from Burke's Station, though he felt sick and exhausted he knew that he had stuck to his post.

After the defeat he was sent to Washington till November 1861 to the headquarters in the War Building, where he had charge of the telegraph department. Here he often came in contact with the great men conducting the war, even President Lincoln himself. Of President Lincoln he wrote :

> Mr. Lincoln would occasionally come to the office and sit at the desk, awaiting replies to telegrams, or perhaps merely anxious for information. When excited, or telling a story, intellect shone through his eyes and illuminated his face to a degree I have seldom seen in any other. His manners were perfect, because natural; and he had a kind word for everybody, even the youngest boy in the office. It was not so much, perhaps, what he said, as the way in which he said it that never failed to win one. I never met a great man who so thoroughly made himself one with all men as Mr. Lincoln. He was the most perfect democrat, revealing in every word and act the equality of men before God !

Abraham Lincoln was indeed a hero to Andrew Carnegie, for they had much in common. Both of them had come from humble homes. Both of them had been poor boys, almost self-taught. Both of them had a passionate love for good books. Both of them had risen largely by their own efforts, and both of them cherished a dream and a hope of raising humanity to happier levels.

In November 1861 Andrew Carnegie was sent back to Pittsburgh, for his services as railroad superintendent were urgently needed there. Soldiers were now passing through the town in hundreds of thousands, as Pittsburgh was one of the greatest railroad centres of the war. It required a capable and energetic man to see to the movement of all these troop-trains, and Andrew was the man for the job. Pittsburgh too was one of the great manufacturing centres of guns and munitions of war. All these had to be safely transported in freight trains to the northern armies on the battlefields. This also came within the scope of Andrew Carnegie's management. He worked night and day keeping things running smoothly.

He was still suffering from headaches as the result of the sunstroke he received during the battle of Bull Run, and with the approaching heat of the summer of 1862 these grew worse. He laboured continually, in poor health, for months, never sparing himself; but in the end the strain proved too great and he collapsed with a serious illness. The doctor ordered a complete rest for three months, and leave of absence was given him by the Pennsylvania Railroad. Andrew was then nearly twenty-seven years old, and this was the first real holiday he had had since he started work as a bobbin boy fourteen years before!

Andrew knew at once where he wanted to spend this long-needed holiday. There was one place he wanted to see more than any other in all the world, and this was Scotland, and in Scotland the most important place for Andrew Carnegie was Dunfermline. It was with tremendous joy that he and his mother looked forward to their visit to the homeland.

CHAPTER 6

A Visit to Scotland

IT WAS TO GEORGE LAUDER, COUSIN DOD OF ANDREW'S
boyhood days in Dunfermline, that Andrew's thoughts first
turned when he knew he was to visit Scotland again. As soon
as he received a letter from the Pennsylvania Railroad Company granting his three months' leave of absence, he wrote
to Dod first of all.

My dear Dod,
    Ten minutes ago I received glorious news. The dream of
a dozen years is at last on the very threshold of realization.
Yes, I am to visit Scotland and see and talk with you all
again, uncles, aunts and cousins, my school-fellows and companions of my childhood—are all to be greeted again. The
past is to be recalled. I shall once more wander through
Woodmill Braes, see Torry and Pitreavie, Limekilns, the
Rumbling Well and a hundred other spots that have haunted
me for years till Dunfermline and its neighbourhood has
grown to be a kind of promised land to me. And all this in
six weeks from now! I can scarcely believe my senses and yet
I'm sure I have just been notified that the Company grants
me three months' leave of absence from July 1st.
    We will make a bee-line for Dunfermline. I won't turn my
head to look at anything until I see Bruce's monument. I
remember that was the last thing I saw of Dunfermline and
I cried bitterly when it could be seen no more . . .
    And now, my dear Dod, good-night. Tell all our friends
we expect to meet them soon, that we look forward to that
long-wished-for day with an intensity of desire felt only by

exiles from home, and with feelings of the warmest friendship for all connected with us in dear Scotland. Good-bye. Let's pray for the early meeting of Dod and Naig.

Truly your affectionate cousin,

ANDREW CARNEGIE.

The Carnegies spent the next month feverishly preparing for the visit to Scotland: Andrew making sure that all his work on the railway was up to date, and that his duties would be carried on properly during his absence; Mrs. Carnegie preparing the necessary clothes and arranging for the care of the house at Homewood.

This trip to Scotland was a triumph indeed for Margaret Carnegie. She had gone to America on borrowed money, with hardly any gear at all, practically penniless. She was going back now in good circumstances, with ample money saved, and her son, still only twenty-six years old, a very important railway official, respected by all, and with the promise of a great career before him. Her second son, still only eighteen, was also doing well under his brother's wing, with the promise of making a success of his career also.

On June 28, 1862 Mrs. Carnegie, Andrew, and Andrew's great friend Tom Miller sailed in the steamship *Etna*, and the voyage took them a fortnight. As soon as they landed in Liverpool they took the train to Dunfermline, not even pausing in Edinburgh except to change trains. As the train rolled towards Dunfermline, Andrew Carnegie felt that he was in a happy dream. Margaret Carnegie sat quietly, gazing through the window, anxious to miss nothing of the loved old places. When she saw the beautiful golden broom crowning the low hills about Dunfermline, she cried, " Oh, there's the broom! The bonnie broom! " and her eyes filled with tears. At last the Abbey Tower of Dunfermline appeared on the horizon, the words KING ROBERT THE BRUCE standing out in huge stone letters to crown it, and the little grey houses of Dunfermline clustering round. After fourteen years of waiting and dreaming, Andrew and his mother stepped out of the train into beloved Dunfermline once more. They both had tears in their eyes, for joy, and a little for sorrow too, at the thought of the dear father who had gone with them from Dunfermline but who would never come back to it.

All their relations were thrilled and delighted to see them again. It was decided that, to please everyone, Mrs. Carnegie should go to stay with her relations, the Morrisons, while Andrew should stay with his dear Uncle Lauder. So, once more Andrew found himself at 8, the High Street, behind the grocer's shop.

Though he was so happy to be back in Scotland, Andrew had a strange sense almost of disappointment in Dunfermline. Everything seemed dwarfed and small to him, the houses, the shops, the school. He was completely puzzled. When he reached Uncle Lauder's he stared round the room and exclaimed, " You are all here. Everything is just as I left it, but over here you all seem to have been playing with toys."

He forgot that though Dunfermline had remained the same in many things, he had grown up from the lad who had wept so bitterly to leave the little grey town, and his eyes were used to the wide sweeps of America's scenery, to the tall gigantic buildings, even to the bigger planning that characterized the expansion of the new land. He was, besides, tired and jaded, in spite of all the joy of his return, and things had fallen a little flat after all the intense excitement. Only the lovely gracious Abbey with the familiar silvery sound of its bell, the beautiful Palace ruin, and the wooded slopes of Pittencrieff Glen seemed to him as glorious and grand as ever.

After a while things began to fall into their true proportions once more and Andrew slipped easily into the delightful renewing of " auld acquaintances ". Uncle Lauder never disappointed him, nor Dod. Andrew wrote of his return to Uncle Lauder's house :

> My home, of course, was with my instructor, guide and inspirer, Uncle Lauder. Now I was nearly twenty-seven, but Uncle Lauder still remained Uncle Lauder. He had not shrunk. No one could fill his place. We had our walks and talks constantly, and I was " Naig " to him again.

Andrew spent a great deal of his visit in looking up his old relations and friends. Uncle Tom Morrison, once a fire-brand, was now a much respected municipal councillor of Dunfermline and gentler than he used to be. Ailie Henderson and her husband, who had lent the Carnegies the money to go to America, had fared quite well, and managed to buy a nice house for themselves in Reid Street. Mr. Martin, Andrew's old schoolmaster, had died, and for this Andrew was very sorry, for he wished to thank Mr. Martin for all his good teaching; but it was a great joy to Andrew to meet many of his school-fellows again.

But after he had been a short time in Dunfermline Andrew caught a severe cold. He had never quite recovered from his illness; chill settled upon his chest, and soon he was desperately ill with pneumonia.

There were no modern methods of treating pneumonia then. The only things that were done to help a patient to recover were to keep him warm and to make him perspire to get rid of the fever. Another remedy for all diseases at this time was to bleed the patient by affixing leeches to his body to suck out a quantity of blood. This very drastic treatment was carried out in Andrew's case, and ill and anaemic as he probably was then, it is a wonder that he ever recovered! There was a toughness in Andrew Carnegie, however, that survived illness as well as hard times. For six weeks he lay in bed in Uncle Lauder's house, and when he did get up he was too weak to stand. A sorry ending to his long-dreamed-of holiday!

Andrew had planned to visit London and the Rhine, and to see some of the lovely mountainous parts of Scotland, but all these ideas had now to be given up. Once he was able to move about, he spent a little time on the shores of Loch Leven trying to recover sufficient health to return to America when his leave was finished. The fortnight's sea voyage helped to restore him, so that he was able to return to his work, but it was a long time before he really threw off the effects of his illness.

On the whole, great as his love was for Dunfermline, Andrew was glad to be back in America again, and the railway men of Pittsburgh were glad to see him return; he was such a capable and hard-working superintendent, understanding so well the men who worked for him. As his train entered Pittsburgh Andrew was surprised to see a crowd of the workmen waiting at the station. As soon as Andrew popped his head out of the carriage window, a shout of cheering went up, and some of the men fired a cannon they had drawn up in readiness.

" What's all this? " Andrew asked Tom Miller in surprise.

" It's for you, Andy. They're welcoming you home like royalty! " Tom Miller laughed.

Andrew never forgot that splendid homecoming, and the warmth of it stayed with him all his days. Straight away he took up his duties on the railway, and they were anxious ones indeed. The Confederates were advancing against the north, and the war for a time wavered to and fro, with the Southern States crying, " On to Washington! " and the Northern States, " On to Richmond! " Between these two cities the great armies swung back and forth, and fierce battles were fought, and again Andrew had to arrange movements of thousands of troops by train.

In 1862 the great oil-fields of Pennsylvania began to attract attention. A year or two earlier a man called Drake had discovered that western Pennsylvania contained great underground lakes of petroleum. The outbreak of war prevented their being developed at first, but once the war had settled into its stride Andrew Carnegie and his friends at Homewood began to be excited about further discoveries that were being made. One of Andrew's older friends, William Coleman, who owned the Pittsburgh Opera House, talked about it when Andrew was visiting him.

" Do you see there's been another strike of oil out west, Andy? At a place called Oil Creek, I understand," he said.

" Yes, I noticed that, Mr. Coleman."

" I hear that men are flocking there already and buying the land round about."

" If the oil can be used for machinery it will be tremendously valuable," Andrew said thoughtfully. " Land there is going to be worth a great deal, once men get up oil in any quantity."

" That's what I think," Mr. Coleman agreed. " Andy, what do you say if we take a trip there and have a look round? I think it might be worth our while to buy some property there,"

" It'll be a rough journey, of course, for there's no railway, but who cares? " Andrew said. " We can go in a horse wagon."

A new adventure always appealed to Andrew, and he loved horses.

" We'll probably have to sleep in the wagon as well," Mr. Coleman pointed out. " What few inns there are will be full of folk, and there are not many private houses."

" We'll take a tent," Andrew suggested, never at a loss. So, almost in the spirit of a camping holiday, Andrew Carnegie and William Coleman set off in their wagon.

Over terrible roads the wagon jolted, along mere tracks that other wagons had made before them, deeply rutted, thick with dust in dry weather, deep in mud when it rained.

Their journey of seventy-five miles took them almost three days, for they had to rest the horses, feed and water them, and set up their tent at night. At last they reached Oil Creek, a small stream that flowed into the Allegheny River, and found a little town of wooden shanties that had sprung up almost over night. All up and down the banks of the river wooden derricks had been erected and men were making borings for oil wells. Everyone was in great spirits, expecting to make a fortune in no time. Mud was everywhere and the little creek was thick and foul with oil that had run to waste from the underground reservoirs. As fast as the buckets at the oil wells brought up oil it was tipped into flat-bottomed boats that leaked badly, and so not only the crew but the Allegheny river was rapidly becoming coated with oil. A great deal of valuable oil was lost by careless handling.

In spite of the hardships of the journey, Mr. Coleman and Andrew enjoyed themselves. They found that several wells had been sunk on the property known as Storey Farm. Here they watched oil gushing up from a well that had been made.

" This is the place, Andy," Mr. Coleman declared in a voice little above a whisper. " If the oil from that well could be piped into a reservoir, we could soon have a small lake of oil and keep it there in reserve. We could sell from it as we required, and by running fresh oil in each day we could keep the reservoir at the same level. Some day the oil in Pennsylvania is bound to be done. It can't last for ever. When supplies begin to fail, then the price will go up. When that time comes, we shall still have a lake with thousands of barrels of oil in it."

" It is certainly a very clever notion," Andrew agreed.

" Would you feel like joining me in buying the farm, Andy? " Mr. Coleman asked. " If we could raise enough money, I think we could persuade the owner to sell it to us."

"There'll be money required for working it, as well as the purchase price," Andrew remarked with his usual shrewdness. "Could we not form a company and ask other people to take shares with us? Tom, my brother, has some money put by, for one; and there's Tom Miller, and one or two other folk at Homewood."

"A good suggestion. How much money do you think we shall need, Andrew?"

"About forty thousand dollars," Andrew said, after making a few calculations. "Of course, we shouldn't need to put down all that sum at once. We could, perhaps, buy an option on the farm for a tenth of that sum, say four thousand dollars at once, and promise the rest of the money within a certain time. That would give us time to organize our company."

"Let us go and talk with the owner of the farm," Mr. Coleman decided.

The owner was willing to part with his farm for what seemed the vast sum of forty thousand dollars, and Andrew Carnegie and Mr. Coleman formed, with their friends, the Columbia Oil Company. Before long a dozen oil-wells were gushing on the property, and the wells continued to yield thousands of barrels of oil *every day* for the next twenty-five years without any sign of running dry. It seemed almost as if there were an underground *sea* of oil.

Andrew bought his share in this company with the profits that the Woodruff Sleeping Cars brought in, and straight away the Columbia Oil Company began to make very great profits indeed. In 1863 the Columbia Oil Company paid Andrew nearly 18,000 dollars, (about £3,600, then) as his share of the profit for one year. Altogether in 1863, from the various companies in which he had shares, and from his salary as superintendent of the railway line, Andrew, then only twenty-eight years old, had an income of 50,000 dollars or about £10,000. That was a wonderful amount for a boy who had arrived in America a penniless lad only fifteen years before. Already Andrew had the touch of gold.

It was about this time, too, that Andrew began to be interested in the iron trade. Pittsburgh was one of the chief homes of iron manufacture in America, and all day smoke poured from its many iron-founding furnaces. With the coming of the Civil War the price of iron went up enormously. Iron was needed for cannon, for guns, for rails to extend the railway tracks, for locomotives. Andrew saw that there was going to be a great demand for iron for a long time.

One of Andrew's great friends on the railway was John L. Piper, the hefty blacksmith-mechanic who ran the repair-shops of the Pennsylvania Railroad. He had charge of all the bridges on the railway. At this time Andrew became very found of horse-riding, and one morning as he was having a ride he passed the repair-shops, where he saw the gigantic figure of John Piper already at work.

" Hullo, John! You're early at it! " he called out.

" Aye! " John exclaimed. " I've a bridge to get repaired or all the traffic on the line will be delayed to-day." He cast a wise glance over Andrew's horse. " That's a good bit of horse-flesh you're riding, Andy," he said approvingly. " You know a good horse right enough! Raised in Kentucky, I'd say that horse was! "

" You're right, John! "

" Aye, you can't beat Kentucky when it comes to horses. Raised on a farm I was, and there's nothing I enjoy better than breaking in a good Kentucky colt. I still keep one or two horses. You must come and see them for yourself some time, Andy."

" I'll be glad to," Andrew said promptly. " You could teach me a lot about horses, John. But right now did you say you'd got a bridge to repair? "

" Aye, my lad, I'm just back from Aliquippa. There's

been a bridge burnt down and the traffic'll be held up for nearly a week till I get a new bridge built. I'll get single line traffic going as quick as I can, though."

" How did it happen? "

" Fire as usual," John Piper said disgustedly. " You get a locomotive going across a wooden bridge. Red-hot cinders fall out of the engine furnace on to the wooden floor of the bridge. Up springs a strong wind and fans the flames. The engine driver passes on, not guessing that anything's wrong, and before he's more than a few miles away, the bridge is ablaze. It happens like that almost every time."

" And there's nothing to be done about it, I suppose," Andrew said thoughtfully. " We can't employ a man to watch every bridge on the line."

" No, but it'll keep on happening all the time as long as bridges are made of wood," John Piper said darkly.

" What would you make them of? " Andrew said quickly. " Iron? "

" Aye, Andy, iron ! "

Andrew looked at him with interest. " But aren't iron bridges apt to break rather easily? "

" Iron's tougher than it used to be," John Piper declared. " There are ways of casting iron now to make it tough. Iron's the thing for bridges, not wood that burns so easily."

" I believe you're right, John. But wouldn't iron bridges be expensive to build? A railroad needs a lot of bridges, you know."

" The bridges could be cast in sections," John Piper told him. " A small bridge would take a few sections, a big one more sections, that is all. But come in here, Andy. I've something I'll show you."

Andrew tethered his horse and followed him. John took him into his own workshop, a little apart from the repair-yards.

106

" There ! " he said in triumph. " That's the first iron bridge manufactured in Pennsylvania."

Andrew stared. There, before him, was a small sectional iron bridge designed to take a single track line over a small stream.

" That's neat, John ! " he said admiringly.

" Yes, it's small, but it's well made, Andy. Linville, the Pennsylvania Railroad's bridge engineer, designed it, and I made it for him. It's a tiny affair but big ones can be made like it. That's the contraption that will carry American railways over difficult places in the future, you'll see ! "

Andrew surveyed the bridge from every angle. " You're right, John. They've been building iron bridges in England for quite a little while now, but there's so much wood in America, and it costs so little."

" It's dear in the long run if the bridges are always being burnt down and swept away by river floods. There'll come a day yet, you'll see, Andy, that all the wooden bridges will disappear."

" I suppose that will happen," Andrew said thoughtfully.

" Bound to ! " John Piper was quite certain. " The whole railroad will have to be rebuilt before long, mark my words, and everywhere iron will take the place of wood."

Andrew did " mark his words," and went away and did some thinking. He decided that a company that made iron bridges would do very well in America, so he invited H. J. Linville, who designed bridges, and John Piper and his partner, Mr. Schiffler, and Mr. Scott, the President of the Pennsylvania Railroad, to have a talk together.

The outcome of it was a new company to build bridges, and they all took a fifth share in it. The company prospered enormously. As Andrew himself said of it, " Tall oaks from little acorns grew." Before long Andrew made his company larger still and called it " The Keystone Bridge Company." Several workshops were erected in Pittsburgh and immediately orders came in for iron bridges, especially from the railway companies. Soon the Keystone Bridge Company was building bridges over the wide Ohio and Mississippi rivers, and Andrew was making a great deal of money out of his bridge building. Keystone Bridges soon got a good name for excellent workmanship. " There was no luck about it," Andrew wrote himself. " We used only the best material and enough of it, making our own iron. We were proud of our bridges. They were *honest* bridges. I have never known a concern to make a decided success that did not do good honest work."

Side by side with all his business concerns went on Andrew's work as the Pittsburgh Superintendent of the Railroad, a big job in itself during those years of Civil War, when so many men and munitions had to be moved quickly from place to place at short notice. At one time Pittsburgh itself was threatened by the Southern armies who were preparing to invade Pennsylvania. They had won battle after battle, and if they could capture the city they would deal a severe blow to the Northern States, a blow that might decide the war.

In June a telegram was sent from the Northern Army Headquarters in Washington, saying that Pittsburgh was in immediate danger and that trenches must be dug at once round the city. Immediately seven thousand men set to work to dig these fortifications. Thirty thousand volunteers were armed and equipped, and it was Andrew's job to transport them by train to the threatened danger points. Even though for a time the situation looked black, Andrew Carnegie, always the optimist, was as certain as ever that the northern forces would win. In a letter to Dod in 1863 he wrote :

You will see by the papers that Pittsburgh is busy fortifying. Volunteers have been at work all week. We will not quit until the city is surrounded by formidable works, and we are secure from rebel raids.

Of course I am as certain as ever that the Government is to emerge triumphant and slavery to go down.

> " Freedom's battle once begun,
> Bequeathed by bleeding sire to son,
> Though baffled oft, is ever won."

It was only about a month later, in July, that the most terrible battle of the Civil War was fought at Gettysburg. For three days the battle swung to and fro through the little town. The third day saw preparations for the last fierce assault. The Northern troops held a range of hills just above the town. On both sides men waited in a terrible silence for the signal that the battle had begun. About one o'clock there was a loud roar of guns and a terrific duel between the cannon. Then, suddenly, the guns of the Northern troops fell silent. The Confederates thought they had silenced the batteries. This was a fatal mistake, for the Northern armies were biding their time.

The Confederates charged the hills on which the Northerners were posted. They dashed across the valley with magnificent courage, but immediately the Northern batteries let loose their cannon with tremendous force, a withering fire that cut down the Confederate armies like corn before a reaper. The assault broke. The men wavered, then fled in all directions : the wild desperate charge had failed, and the Confederates had lost the day. They had lost even more : they had lost the war, for the best of their manhood had gone in that fearful charge. They were short of men, munitions, money and supplies. For a year the war dragged on, but it was plain that the Northern States were the victors and in April, 1865, the end came.

When there was no doubt that the war was to be over in a few days, Andrew Carnegie took a step he had been thinking of for some time. His own affairs and the companies in which he was interested were taking more and more of his time. He resigned his post with the Pennsylvania Railroad so that he could be more at liberty to launch out into business; the business that was beginning to hold him more and more, iron manufacture. From now on, Carnegie's name was to be linked with the great growth of iron and steel works in America. Andrew was looking ahead to the future.

CHAPTER 7

Andrew Carnegie Launches Out

FROM THE DAY THAT ANDREW CARNEGIE LEFT THE Pennsylvania Railroad, he never worked again for a salary. He was always a man of business conducting his own affairs. He was then thirty years old.

At this time America was beginning to extend westwards towards the Pacific. As each new state began to be developed, towns were built and these linked to each other by railways. Andrew Carnegie was a far-seeing man and he realized that many miles of railway lines would be required. For these iron rails would have to be made, so in 1864, before he even left the railway, Andrew started a foundry or iron rolling mills, the Union Iron Mills. He became an ironmaster, and his business grew quickly as the railroads extended.

As the lines of rails grew in number and length, more locomotives were also required. Andrew foresaw this too, and in 1866 he founded the Pittsburgh Locomotive Works. His motto was still " Make nothing but the very best ", and his products earned a name for great reliability. Andrew was well on the way to becoming a very rich man indeed.

The next year, 1867, he had his affairs so well organized that he felt he could afford to take a holiday in Europe. With him went Henry Phipps, the son of Mr. Phipps, the shoemaker who had given employment to Mrs. Carnegie when the Carnegies first settled in America. This time Andrew had a wonderful trip and visited most of the capitals of Europe. Andrew said they "had climbed every spire, slept on mountain tops, and carried our luggage in knapsacks on our backs."

A special treat to Andrew was a visit to the Crystal Palace in London, where a musical festival, the Handel Anniversary, was being celebrated. He was very fond of listening to good orchestral music. During his visits abroad, too, he was always looking out for new methods of iron manufacture and bringing back new ideas for his Union Mills at Pittsburgh.

In 1867 Tom Carnegie married Lucy Coleman. It was decided that Tom and Lucy should take over the Carnegie's house at Homewood while Andrew and his mother should move to New York.

There were two reasons for this move; first, the expansion of the iron-works and other great businesses that Andrew had started, like the Pittsburgh Locomotive Works, meant that someone ought to attend to money matters in New York. Andrew was the most suitable person. The other reason was a more personal one. Now he was so rich, Andrew, at last, had time to "play." He himself felt the need of yet more education. He wanted more time and opportunity for reading, for music, for art. He wanted to develop that side of his nature which he felt had been neglected in youth. Always fond of writing and expressing his own personal opinions, he also wanted time to write books. He decided to spend the mornings at business, and to give the afternoons to these pursuits.

At first Andrew and his mother felt rather lost in New York without their Pittsburg friends; and Mrs. Carnegie missed her garden and her country walks. Instead of buying a house, they went to live in an hotel, at first the St. Nicholas Hotel on Broadway. This was the most palatial hotel in New York, with marble stairways, lofty ceilings, crystal chandeliers, walls hung with mirrors and tapestries, and

112

deep thick carpets. Mrs. Carnegie felt she was living in a palace.

" I mind well the first time your father and I walked up Broadway," she told Andrew. " I had you by the hand and your father carried Thomas. How we stared about us as we passed this place, and I tried to peep in through the door. Little did I dream then that one day I should live here myself." The strangeness soon wore off for Mrs. Carnegie, who began to enjoy the comfort and splendour of her new surroundings.

It was at this time, in 1868, that Andrew Carnegie began to think about himself and the future and the great wealth he was beginning to acquire. He made a few notes then about his personal dreams and ambitions, and this paper was found among his possessions manys years afterwards. Among other things it said :

> Thirty-three and an income of 50,000 dollars a year. Beyond this never earn—make no effort to increase fortune, but spend the surplus each year for benevolent purposes. Cast business aside for ever, except for others.
>
> Settle in Oxford and get a thorough education, making the acquaintance of literary men—this will take three years' active work—pay special attention to speaking in public.
>
> Settle then in London, taking a part in public matters, especially those connected with education and improvement of the poorer classes.
>
> Man must have an idol, but no idol is more debasing than the worship of money. To continue much longer overwhelmed by business cares, and with most of my thoughts upon the way to make more money in the shortest time, must degrade me beyond hope of recovery. I will resign business at thirty-five, but during the next two years I wish to spend the afternoons in receiving instruction and in reading.

Though many years were to pass before Andrew could

devote himself to carrying out this programme, yet in large part he did carry it out before he died. He was never able to study at Oxford and that part of his dream had to go. Neither did he go to live in London. Later on, though, he was to do more than any other single man to bring reading and education within the reach of the poorer classes. He did study the art of public speaking, and he did spend a great deal of his spare time in reading and studying. In education, as well as in business, Andrew Carnegie was a self-made man.

As he grew older and richer, Andrew was to think even more deeply about his great wealth, and the idea began to grow in him that he held it in trust for other people, so that with it he might bring happiness and wisdom to other men. He was to put these ideas into action later on, but something happened to make Andrew Carnegie change his mind about retiring from business. This was the beginning of the age of steel.

Steel was not a new thing. It had been used for some time for fine swords, razors, needles, scissors, pocket knives and cutlery. It was so expensive that only small articles were made of it. Steel is tougher than cast-iron; it bends, but it does not easily break. The cost in fuel to produce steel at that time, however, was enormous.

In 1856 an inventor named Bessemer was trying to find an inexpensive way of making steel. He found that the worst impurity in iron was carbon. For two years he worked among his experimental furnaces to find a cheap way to get rid of the carbon : at last, almost by chance, he stumbled on the solution.

He found that several pieces of pig-iron (crude iron), which had been heated, had been subjected to blasts of cold air. These pieces of iron were almost free of carbon. What had happened was that the oxygen in the cold air had united with the carbon in the molten iron and changed it

114

into a gas. In the intense heat the carbon was driven off and destroyed.

Bessemer next invented his " converter ", a huge vessel, steel on the outside, lined with fire-brick on the inside. In the bottom were little chimneys through which cold air could be blown through the molten iron in the converter. The oxygen in the air forced into the converter raised the molten iron to a great heat and the carbon was driven off in a great white flame that shot high into the air. When the molten metal was run out from the converter into moulds, it was steel.

On one of his English visits in 1872 Andrew Carnegie made the acquaintance of Henry Bessemer. Bessemer explained to him how his converter worked, and let him see one in action. When Andrew Carnegie saw the dazzling flame from the converter carry off the impurities, and the fine quality of the steel that remained after the air had been blasted through it, he had only one idea; to introduce the Bessemer process of making steel into his own iron-mills at Pittsburgh.

He was shown a Bessemer steel rail in the Camden Goods Yard. In four years this rail showed no signs of wear, splitting or cracking, while the iron rails laid alongside it had been renewed seventeen times! This decided Carnegie. He knew that the iron rails on American railways wore away very quickly and often had to be replaced. Soon a big number of new railways would be built to reach the Pacific coast, and they would use powerful heavy locomotives. The wear on the rails would be terrific. Only steel rails would be the answer to this problem. Carnegie resolved that he must be the first in America to manufacture steel rails in a big way.

He dashed back to America on the first steamer he could take and hurried to Pittsburgh. There he burst into the office of Carnegie, Kloman and Company and cried, " The day of iron has passed. Steel is king ! "

His partners stared at him in astonishment.

" We must go in for the manufacture of steel rails and start at once ! "

Tom Carnegie, Henry Phipps and Andrew Kloman had no enthusiasm for Andrew's new plans, however.

" That would cost a mint of money, Andrew," Henry Phipps told him

" We are doing pretty well as it is," Tom pointed out. " Steel might or might not prove a success. We do know where we are with iron."

" We don't know anything about making steel, either, Andy," Phipps added.

" It would be foolish to make changes. We might lose all our money," Andrew Kloman declared.

" Iron will have to make way for steel, you will see," Andrew warned them. " Why, iron rails have to be re-newed on the railways every few months. I've seen steel rails in England that will last almost for ever."

" But if it lasts for ever, Andrew, we should be doing our-selves an ill turn in making it. Quite a lot of our business is in renewing iron rails on the railroads, remember."

"Aye, but look a bit further ahead, Harry," Andrew replied. " Any railroad that is worth the name will be replacing its iron rails by these new steel rails, and before very long, either. We want to be the first in the American market."

" You always like to take time by the forelock, don't you, Andy ? "

" Aye, but it's the only road to success, Tom; to look a jump ahead of the next man ! "

All his persuasion, however, could not move his three partners to take up the business of manufacturing steel in place of iron. When Andrew saw that they were not to be convinced of the wisdom of this move, he said, " Very well! I shall start a separate company with other partners, for I am determined to go into the steel business."

Andrew Carnegie did get other men to join with him in this new enterprise. One of his chief partners was J. Edgar Thomson, who was President of the Pennsylvania Railroad when Andrew was employed in it as a young telegraph clerk. Andrew decided to build big new steel furnaces and rolling mills, and out of respect for Mr. Thomson (and also, truth to tell, because Mr. Thomson purchased many tons of equipment for the railway) Andrew named his new steel works the Edgar Thomson Steel Company, Limited. Andrew chose an excellent position for his steel mills, where two railways, the Pennsylvania Railroad and the Baltimore and Ohio Railroad, met by the Ohio river. It would be easy for the new steel company to supply the needs of both these great systems.

While the new works was still being built there was a sudden panic in the business world of the United States. Many businesses went bankrupt or had no money to carry on. One factory after another closed down and there were many unemployed workers. People could not pay their bills. In Pittsburgh many iron-works had to stop their smelting, and the furnaces went cold. No smoke came from the mill chimneys, and work-people wandered the Pittsburgh streets, wondering where they would get the money to pay for their next meal. The banks closed their doors and refused to pay out any money at all.

The Texas Pacific Railway, in which Andrew Carnegie had a large number of shares, had to stop building and the company went bankrupt. Whispers began to go round that Andrew Carnegie and his partners would not have enough money to finish the new steel works they were building. Bank managers who had lent money towards the new works began to think they could not lend Carnegie any more, for fear he went bankrupt too, and had no money to repay what he had borrowed from them.

When these ugly rumours reached Carnegie's ears he was in New York but he went at once to Pittsburgh. At a meeting called by the bank manager of the Exchange Bank of Pittsburgh, he explained his position to them. There he sat, a small fair-haired slight figure, in his chair at the long table round which the bank officials took their places.

" Mr. Carnegie, we have heard that your friends, Mr. Thomson and Mr. Scott, have lost money heavily on the Texas Railway. We know you were connected with them in business and we understand that you have shares in the Texas Railway too," the bank manager said.

" Yes, I am a shareholder in that railway," Andrew told him calmly. " I had 250,000 dollars in it." (That was about £50,000 in the money of that day.)

" And have you borrowed the money from any bank to pay for those shares? "

" Gentlemen, I never buy a share in any business for which I have not the means to pay," Andrew told them firmly. " If I borrow money from a bank I have always other possessions or shares that I can sell to pay that bank, if need arises. All my shares in the Texas Railway have already been paid for. I owe no money for them at all, or for shares in any other company either. I stand clear and clean."

The bank manager breathed a sigh of relief. " You will, of course, lose your money in the Texas Railway? " he said cautiously.

" I don't know about that," Andrew replied at once with his usual optimism. " I might lose the money, but I don't think so. The United States is a big country and it must expand its communications. This railway is sure to be needed before long. It might suffer a set-back, but time will show. Even if I do lose that money, I own many other

118

shares in other companies that are all paid for, and I shall not be much affected."

"But what about the Edgar Thomson works you are building?" one man asked him.

"Sir, every dollar I possess, every piece of property that is mine, every share in any company that I own, I am willing to sell to put into my new steel company, for I have faith in it. Gentlemen," Andrew turned to the rest of the company, "I believe in putting all my eggs in one basket *and watching that basket*. As soon as I can arrange matters, work will begin again on my new steel mills."

Andrew was as good as his word. He sold many of his shares that were still doing well, such as the Sleeping Car Company shares, and poured money into the building of the Edgar Thomson Steel Works. Everywhere else in Pittsburgh iron mills stood desolate, the furnace fires out, all work at a standstill, but Andrew went on building his fine new works, though people shook their heads and said he would lose everything.

Andrew Carnegie knew what he was doing, however. At this time of industrial slackness, both materials and men's labour were cheaper than at any other time. It cost him less to build his works then, than if iron manufacturers had been flourishing all round him. Andrew knew too that after each period when trade was bad, sooner or later things improved and prosperity returned. He was sure that in a great growing country like America new railways would be built and his steel would certainly be required. When trade began to revive he would be ready with his fine new steel works to supply steel rails wherever they were wanted.

His faith in his plans was quite justified. When the Edgar Thomson Steel Works began production in 1875, it made a profit of 11,000 dollars the first *month*! Andrew had indeed launched out into the business that was to bring him more wealth than anything he had tackled yet. It was to this great courage in going ahead when other men faltered that Andrew owed much of his success. There was another person in the Carnegie family who had been prepared to take chances when everything seemed black, and that was Margaret Carnegie. Like mother, like son!

As progress moved westward in America, it moved with Andrew Carnegie's locomotives, on Andrew Carnegie's steel rails. Andrew was tremendously busy organizing his new steel works and getting orders for steel, so that, for a time, his dream of helping mankind with his surplus wealth had to wait; but it was never forgotten, and Andrew kept all these things in his heart till the time was ripe.

Side by side with the building-up of his steel trade Andrew enlarged his own education by reading and by travelling abroad. He had visited Europe more than once. He was able to take these journeys because he had chosen excellent men to take charge of his affairs at the Edgar Thomson works. There was William Borntrager, a young German, whom Carnegie put in charge of the steel rolling mills. William was so devoted to his work that he even grudged taking time off to go to Germany to marry his wife!

Another man whom Andrew Carnegie promoted was a Welshman, Captain Bill Jones. He came to the new steel works as a mechanic earning two dollars a day. From the age of ten years Bill Jones had worked in iron and later in steel mills. He had made every kind of iron goods from railway axles to ploughs. He invented various improvements to the Bessemer Converter, and even Henry Bessemer himself said that Bill Jones knew more about steel than any man in the United States. Captain Jones and Andrew Carnegie got on extremely well together. They were both fond of literature and of writing, too. Captain Jones became superintendent of the Edgar Thomson works. Andrew Carnegie always called him Bill, and to him Andrew became Andy.

Captain Jones did so well for the steel company that Andrew wanted to reward him by making him a partner in it. Andew always tried to give men who worked well for him a share in the profits of his business. He called Captain Jones into his office.

" Bill, we have decided to give you a share in the business. We are going to set aside some shares in your name. You will not have to pay for them, but as the profits on the shares come in, they will go to pay for your shares. As the company is doing well and piling up profits, it won't be long before the shares are absolutely yours."

" That's mighty nice of you, Andy, and thanks very much," Bill said. " But do you mind if I think it over first, please? "

Andrew Carnegie was surprised, but he gave Bill Jones time to consider whether he would accept his offer or not. Next day Bill Jones came back to him.

" It's no use, Andy, I'm just a plain workman," he said. " I've got great influence over the men, I know, but it's because I've been a mechanic like them before I became superintendent. If you make me a partner they'll think I've risen far above them. That way I shan't be able to control them as I always have."

" Oh, but we've got to recognize your good work in some way, Bill," Andrew cried, disappointed. " What do you suggest, then? "

Captain Bill thought for a minute. " Well, you could pay me a durned big salary," he declared.

Andrew Carnegie laughed aloud and slapped the lid of his desk. " I'll do it! " he declared. " How would you like the same salary as the President of the United States, Bill? "

" Ah, well, Andy, now you're talking ! "

So, to everyone's surprise Bill Jones was paid the same money as the President of the United States! If Carnegie worked his men hard and expected them to give him their best, he also knew how to reward them very generously.

Besides Europe Carnegie visited Japan and China. He did not care much for Japan, which he said was " too much like a toy-shop ", and he did not like her warlike attitude. He much preferred China, where a man was respected for being a scholar and not a soldier.

The trip which gave him, perhaps, the greatest joy of all was one that he and his mother took in 1881, when Andrew organized a *coaching* party through Britain, and that meant a stage-coach drawn by horses.

Andrew invited a party of friends to go with him on his coaching tour. He had a beautiful red and black coach specially built. His driver and footman wore blue and silver liveries, and the footman sounded a silver horn at the times of departure. The coach was drawn by four sleek bay horses, their harness polished and glossy, the buckles glistening in the sun. Andrew chose ten friends, ladies and gentlemen, to go with him. In the front seat, beside her son, Mrs. Carnegie sat, wearing a plain black dress and bonnet. Mrs. Carnegie always saw to it that she had the seat next to Andrew, for there were one or two unmarried ladies in the party who might have set their caps at Andrew, and Mrs. Carnegie was plainly having no nonsense of that kind! Andrew was now a very wealthy man, and well worth having as a husband, but Mrs. Carnegie always stood on guard like a dragon over him. As she grew older she became more and more possessive and looked on Andrew as her own property. She felt she must protect him from any designing young ladies! It is very doubtful, though, if Andrew Carnegie would have married while his mother was alive. To him she had always been his heroine, the one who had given him his great chances in life, and gratitude was one of the strongest of Andrew's characteristics.

The coaching trip was to last seven weeks, and they were to journey from Brighton to Inverness. Andrew Carnegie really wanted his mother to see Scotland again, for she was now nearly seventy-one years old; he had never forgotten his promise that some day she should ride in her own carriage through the streets of Dunfermline, and this time he was determined to make his dream come true.

It was a very merry party indeed that took the road to the north, and Andrew Carnegie was the life and soul of it all. Each morning the horn called the company to the coach and they took their places on top with a splendid view of the country about them. Sometimes they picnicked in a wood or beside a stream; sometimes they stopped to look at a cathedral or some historic place, and every night they slept at a beautiful country inn. People were on the look-out for Andrew's coach and four, and as they swung through the villages children ran out and waved to them and gave them a cheer. Even Mrs. Carnegie dropped her rather grim manner and became gay with the young folk. She gave up her front seat and took one in the back row among the young ladies, where Andrew declared, " Her tongue went from morning till night, if I do say it, and her end of the coach was always in for its share of every frolic going."

Once, when the coach stopped so they could have a picnic beside a stream among the hills, Mrs. Carnegie took off her shoes and stockings and paddled " like any wee lassie." Once she even kilted up her long black skirts and danced a Highland dance on the green banks of a river. Even devoted Andrew wrote of this—though a little in admiration, " To be a wee lassie at seventy-one is a triumph indeed. We were all daft enough while coaching, but Mother really ought to have been restrained a little. She

123

went beyond all bounds! " In his secret heart Andrew was very proud of her.

So, through the lovely heart of England, through Shakespeare's countryside, over the rolling Pennines, by the crags and shining waters of the Lake District, the coach made its way, and at last, in July, the happy party sighted the lovely rounded hills of southern Scotland, and cheering gaily dashed across the Border.

After a visit had been paid to Ayr and the country where Robert Burns had lived, they headed straight for Edinburgh and Dunfermline. At Edinburgh they stayed a day longer than they had intended, for there Andrew received a telegram asking him to postpone his arrival in Dunfermline for a day. Great preparations were evidently afoot!

Andrew waited for a day, then his gay coach crossed the Forth to North Queensferry, where the party stopped for lunch at the inn there. The landlady threw up her hands in horror at seeing this large and unexpected party descend upon her for a meal.

" I'm all alone. There's nobody in the house! The lasses are all away to Dunfermline, for there's great goings-on there the day! "

" Couldn't you manage some sort of a meal for us? " Andrew coaxed.

" Well, there's cold meat in the larder, and eggs, but who's to set the tables? " she said doubtfully.

" We'll *all* help you! " the coaching party declared, and so they did, rummaging in the larder themselves and carrying plates and knives and forks through to the dining-room. Andrew himself began to tremble a little with fearful joy at the thought of the " goings on " that awaited them in Dunfermline.

Just as they were about to mount the coach again, a white-haired active figure came hastening along the road.

" Uncle Lauder ! " Andrew called in delight and ran to meet him.

" Aye, Andrew lad, it's me, right enough," Uncle Lauder said, kissing Mrs. Carnegie and shaking hands warmly with Andrew. " I felt I had to be with you when you entered Dunfermline. I just couldn't wait for you to come."

" Up on to the coach with you, Uncle Lauder ! " Andrew said. " Sit beside me. I want to talk to you." He was overjoyed to have the dear uncle and companion of his boyhood days with him on his great entry into Dunfermline.

" To tell you the truth I feel a bit nervous, Uncle Lauder. What are all these goings-on in Dunfermline that we hear about ? "

" No need to be nervous, Andrew. You're going among friends, lad, and they're preparing a warm welcome for you, that's all. The folk are making it a holiday."

The horn sounded and the coach and horses started up the long hill towards Dunfermline. Soon the tower of the Abbey appeared above the skyline.

" Dunfermline, Mother ! Dunfermline ! " Andrew cried. " You're back at last, and riding into your dear old town in your own carriage, just as I promised you."

Andrew's hand clasped his mother's, and her eyes misted with tears. " It's like a fairy tale come true," she whispered. " Oh, if only your father had lived to see this day ! " Andrew's grip on her hand strengthened. She might have wept, but just then the unusual appearance of the town caught her eye. Instead of the old bare grey walls, there appeared everywhere masses of flags and bunting. Dunfermline was one blaze of colour in the July sunshine; everywhere the Scottish Lion, the Union Jack and the Stars and Stripes together. There were great banners stretched across the main street with WELCOME CARNEGIE upon them.

On Bothwell Street, where they entered Dunfermline,

It was indeed a triumph for Andrew Carnegie

there was a triumphal arch bedecked with flags and flowers. Here the Provost and the Town Council assembled, all wearing their chains of office, to greet Andrew and his party. As the coach came along brass bands blared their welcome, and the sound of the bagpipes rose from the kilted pipers. A cheer came from the waiting crowd of over twenty thousand people, and echoed along the packed streets in waves of sound.

All the pavements were solid with folk, every window filled, and boys even perched on the rooftops. All Dunfermline was out to give its famous son a warm welcome.

The coach with its splendid horses pulled up at the gay archway, and Andrew and his mother descended and were received by the Provost with warm hand-shaking. Then Andrew was presented with an illuminated address by a member of the Weavers' Guild. He spoke simply and kindly, but at his mention of the old days when the Carnegies had lived in Dunfermline, Margaret Carnegie thought again about her husband, William, and the tears were not far away.

Once more Andrew and his mother took their seats on the gay red and black coach with its shiny metal-work and its four bay horses, and a great procession lined up behind them. First came the various Guilds, the Oddfellows in uniform, the Foresters arrayed in green, then the Gardeners' Guild with their fine banner. After them lined up the workers from the linen factories, the Bleachers, the Weavers, the Dyers, and many other trades. Thousands of women and girls from the linen mills, all dressed in white frocks and carrying British and American flags, made a colourful sight. The procession was more than a mile long! Dunfermline had certainly gone gay.

Whenever Andrew's coach came in sight, a great burst of cheering came from the dense crowds along the streets.

"There he is, on the top of the coach, see!" one man cried. "Yon's Andra Carnegie."

"What! Yon wee man?" his neighbour cried in surprise.

The procession went along the Netherton Broad Street and then turned up into Moodie Street towards the small cottage where Andrew Carnegie had been born. Here, for a minute, the coach stopped and even the cheering crowd was silent. Mrs. Carnegie's heart was very full.

"Andrew! I canna speak!" she faltered. "To think that's where you were born—where your father and I were so happy——"

"Steady, Mother! You mustn't weep now, or you'll have me weeping too!"

Just then the Abbey bell began tolling softly, a lovely silvery sound. This proved too much for Andrew, this sweet sound from the days of his childhood, the sound of the bell that he had kept in his heart all these years. He gulped hard, trying to restrain the tears that could not be held back. "I can't go on—I must give in——" He turned his head aside.

This time it was Mrs. Carnegie who rallied him. "Come, Andrew. You must go on, lad. No one will think the worse of you for a few honest tears."

No one did. Indeed, the crowd cheered in sympathy, and very few eyes among them were dry. It was indeed a day of triumph for Andrew Carnegie, the day when he fulfilled his boyhood promise to his mother that she should ride in her own coach through the streets of Dunfermline for all the folk to see; the day when his own folk of Dunfermline greeted him with all the warmth of their affection and admiration.

For several days Andrew remained in Dunfermline, revisiting old scenes, making speeches, attending ceremonial dinners. The highlight of all that visit, though, was when his mother laid the foundation stone of the new Carnegie Library which was being built in Abbot Street, and which Andrew had given to the city.

The Provost had asked Andrew Carnegie if he would lay the foundation stone himself, but Andrew replied, " Ask my mother, please. I would far rather the honour went to her. My father was one of five weavers who founded the earliest lending library in this town. He did it just by lending his precious books to neighbours. As he and his friends bought books which they could hardly afford, they passed them round to each other. You might, indeed, call it the first circulating library in Dunfermline." He laughed a little proudly. " Yes, ask my mother. She should be the one to do it."

" We shall call the library the Carnegie Library," the Provost informed him. He beckoned to the architect. " The architect would like to have a word with you about it, Mr. Carnegie."

The architect stepped forward. " It is just that the people of Dunfermline would be honoured if we might carve your coat-of-arms over the door, Mr. Carnegie," he said.

Andrew stared at him. " But I have no coat-of-arms, sir ! " he exclaimed. " As you know, I am a simple man, not of noble birth. I am sorry to disappoint you. Instead, however, I should like you to carve a rising sun shedding its rays on the world, with the text beneath it, ' Let there be Light.' "

Margaret Carnegie was proud indeed to lay the foundation stone of the first Carnegie Library. Wearing a fine black silk dress and bonnet ornamented with shining jet, she spread a little mortar with a silver trowel, then tapped the stone with a mallet, and announced in her clear firm voice, " I pronounce this foundation stone well and truly laid, and may God bless the undertaking."

God did indeed bless the undertaking, for this library was the first of many *thousands* of Carnegie Libraries that were to follow it all over the English-speaking world. Like the parent library in Dunfermline, each one was to carry the rising sun in stone, with the words beneath, " Let there be light." It was a fitting and proper thing that Andrew Carnegie should give the first of his many libraries to the place where he had been born. He had never forgotten his own hunger for books as a lad in Pittsburgh, and how Colonel Anderson had supplied his need. Now Andrew had lighted a lamp of learning in Dunfermline that was to find reflections all over the world. These were indeed the days when Andrew Carnegie launched out, not only in steel manufactures, but in the greatness of his giving.

CHAPTER 8

Great Changes

DURING HIS JOURNEYS ABROAD ANDREW CARNEGIE HAD kept diaries, putting down each day all the things he had seen, and his thoughts and feelings about them. Andrew had always wished to be a writer. There was a time when he was young when he would have liked to be a reporter on the staff of a newspaper. He wrote notes of his world tour and made them into a book which he called *Round the World*, and which he had printed just for his friends, and not for sale.

In the same way, as he went through Britain in his splendid red and black coach, he wrote an account of each day's events in a number of twopenny notebooks. One very bad wintry day after his return to America he decided not to go to his New York office, but to stay in his rooms at the Windsor Hotel. To pass the time he took out his notes and began to write another book from them, *An American Four-in-Hand in Britain*. When the book was finished, he asked a publisher, Scribner, to have the book printed just for gifts to his many friends. To his surprise, Scribner suggested that he should print a larger number of copies and sell them to the general public, and pay Andrew a share of the money from the sale. Andrew agreed. Indeed, he admitted that he did not take much persuading, for he had always wanted to see his name in print as the author of a real book. This book proved very popular indeed, for it was written in simple fashion and in such a spirit of enjoyment that the reader shared happily in all Andrew's experiences. So, besides being an important steelmaster, Andrew also became an author. He began to spend more and more time writing, especially articles for famous newspapers. His writing began to make new friendships for him among other authors, poets and statesmen. Andrew began to move in a new literary world.

Among one of the special friends he made was the great Matthew Arnold. The two men met at a dinner party in London. Matthew Arnold was thinking of visiting the United States to give lectures there, and Andrew Carnegie did his best to persuade him to come.

When Matthew Arnold arrived in New York with his wife and daughter, Andrew Carnegie went to the ship to meet them and took them to stay at the Windsor Hotel. For several years now the Carnegies had made their winter home in a suite of rooms in this luxurious hotel, and though Andrew sometimes hinted that he might like a house of his own, Mrs. Carnegie was content to stay where she was, and his mother's wishes were always law to Andrew. Truth to tell, Mrs. Carnegie had grown used in her old age to the easier life of the hotel, and she found it far less exhausting than organizing a household and directing servants. She was also getting more frail in health, and Andrew liked to spare her all he could. Mrs. Carnegie tried to make her home in the hotel as much like a Scottish house as possible. She even had the rooms papered in tartan, probably in imitation of Queen Victoria's rooms in Balmoral Castle! Matthew Arnold took an instant liking to the blunt straightforward Scotswoman, as she did to him.

When Matthew Arnold gave his first lecture in a very large hall in New York, however, it was a complete failure. Though folk could see his lips move, his voice did not reach past the front row of the audience! Every now and again someone from the audience would call out, " We cannot hear you, Mr. Arnold," and Matthew Arnold would raise his voice for a moment, only to drop it again. People began to get up and go home.

When the party got back to the Windsor Hotel, Matthew Arnold asked, " Well, what have you to say? Tell me, will I do as a lecturer? "

" I'm sorry, Mr. Arnold, but it has *not* been a success," Andrew replied, preferring to be truthful even if the great man was offended.

" Do you think, then, that I had better give up my lecture tour? "

" No, but I do not think it would be wise for you to go on till you have had some lessons in public speaking in a large hall," Andrew said without hesitation.

Matthew Arnold turned to Mrs. Carnegie, " And what do *you* think of my first lecture in America, Mrs. Carnegie? "

" Too ministerial! Too ministerial, Mr. Arnold," the blunt old lady declared at once.

" I think you have hit the nail on the head," Matthew Arnold admitted quite frankly.

Matthew Arnold did take Andrew's practical advice and had some lessons in voice production from a professor of elocution, and immediately began to improve.

" Arnold is now a success," Andrew wrote to his friend John Morley, the Member of Parliament for Newcastle. " Everyone can hear him and all is going well now."

Andrew Carnegie spent a short but happy holiday with Matthew Arnold at Andrew's summer cottage at Cresson, a lovely place in the Allegheny mountains, and their friendship grew. There was something about the direct blunt little Scotsman that appealed to Matthew Arnold's honest mind, and the steel manufacturer and the poet found they had a great deal in common.

The next year Andrew Carnegie repeated his coaching trip, this time along the south coast of England. This time

Margaret Carnegie did not go with her son, for her health was beginning to fail. The next autumn of 1886 she was unable to leave their mountain home at Cresson, and Andrew travelled backward and forward from New York to visit her. One day he arrived at Cresson looking very ill.

" My, Andy, but you look fevered! " Mrs. Carnegie exclaimed on seeing him.

" I've not been at all well for a day or two before I left New York. I've had a lot of headache and I just don't seem to want any food. I feel very tired all the time, too."

" I think you're sickening for something," Mrs. Carnegie decided at once. " We'll call the doctor in."

It was as well she did, for when the doctor came he found that Andrew had typhoid fever. This was very dangerous and called for special nursing. A famous New York doctor was called in, and he insisted that Andrew should have a doctor and a nurse attending him all the time. Too much depended on this little Scottish wizard of the steel industry to take any risks at all.

Misfortune came upon misfortune. No sooner had Andrew taken to his bed than news came that his brother Tom was seriously ill with pneumonia in Pittsburgh; and three days later he died. Mrs. Carnegie was never told that he had died, for she herself was sick with worry for her two dear sons; she had a bad heart attack, and was lying in the next room to Andrew. Though the doctor tried to keep the sad news of his mother's serious illness from Andrew, he was so close to her in mind and spirit that he guessed how near to death she was. All that night the early winter snow fell about their frame house at Cresson. In the small hours of the early morning Andrew woke suddenly to find his doctor moving quietly about his room.

" Why are you up so very late? " he asked. " It is long past midnight."

" I was needed for your mother," the doctor told him

quietly.

" But you are not with her now? "

" No. She has no need of me now," the doctor said. " Mr. Carnegie, prepare yourself for a great shock. Your mother passed away a short time ago. It was very peaceful."

Andrew could only shake his head in great sorrow, and turn his face away, too ill and weak to say more.

For a little time after this Andrew's own life trembled in the balance. He was so very ill and in such sad spirits that he seemed to have no wish to recover. Of all that loving and united family, he was the last Carnegie left; his father gone; Tom called away so young, and now his dear mother had left him too. Andrew said afterwards, " I felt the loneliest man in the world."

There was one ray of brightness and comfort, however, to which Andrew turned. For some years he had counted among his great friends a lady who was twenty years younger than himself, the daughter of one of his acquaintances. She was Louise Whitfield, whom Andrew had watched growing up from a schoolgirl, and to whom he had grown very attached. For many years Andrew Carnegie had spent a part of his leisure each day in riding. About this he wrote, " For several years I had known Miss Louise Whitfield. Her mother permitted her to ride with me in the Central Park. We were both very fond of riding. Other young ladies were on my list, too," Andrew admitted. " I had fine horses and often rode in the park and around New York with one or other of the circle. In the end the others all faded into ordinary beings. Miss Whitfield remained alone as the perfect one beyond any I had met."

Though Andrew Carnegie would have liked to marry her some years earlier, there were several obstacles in the way. Truth to tell, the greatest was his own mother. As she was getting old and frail and Andrew felt he owed so much to her, he did not want to hurt her feelings by getting married.

Strong in everything else, Andrew always put his mother's wishes and desires before his own, and it was plain she did not want him to marry.

Louise Whitfield also had her responsibilities. Her father had died, and though her family was very well-to-do, her mother was ill and needed Louise's help to bring up the younger members of the family. In those days the duties of children to their parents often had to take first place. Andrew Carnegie and Louise Whitfield still continued to write very friendly letters to each other.

As soon as Andrew was well enough to write at all, it was to Louise Whitfield he wrote first. He told her of his great loneliness and that he was shortly to be removed to New York, to the care of a famous doctor there, and he begged her to visit him.

For a long time Louise Whitfield had loved Andrew Carnegie in her quiet fashion, in spite of the big difference in their ages. She went to visit him at the nursing home, and when he asked her to marry him, her heart was very willing. They were married in April, 1887, and sailed for Britain straight away for a grand tour.

Andrew was very anxious that all his friends should meet his wife, so very charming and young. They went first to the Isle of Wight, and Uncle Lauder was so anxious to see Andrew's bride that, old as he was, he couldn't wait till they went to Dunfermline, but rushed south by train to meet them. Louise at once won his heart.

" I'm surprised she married ye, Naig! " he declared.

" I'm quite surprised too, Uncle Lauder! " Andrew agreed, laughing.

Although Andrew Carnegie was now fifty-one and his wife only twenty-nine, theirs was a very happy marriage, for Andrew was as young as ever at heart, and as full of plans and the enjoyment of living as he had ever been. He now was the friend of great men, and he introduced his wife to

136

many famous people. They visited Mr. and Mrs. Gladstone in London. They stayed with Lord Rosebery and with John Morley too. Then they travelled north to Dunfermline, the goal of all Andrew's journeys.

On the way north they made a brief stay in Edinburgh, where Andrew was honoured with the Freedom of the City, an honour given only to the most distinguished visitors. While he was there Andrew Carnegie laid the foundation stone of the Central Library on George IV Bridge. Again Andrew was cheered to the echo by thousands of people. After a few days in Dunfermline, they went to Kilgraston Castle, which they had rented for the summer.

Here Andrew entertained his friends in great style, with a Highland piper to wake them each morning by playing the pipes, and a coach and four horses to take them on excursions and twenty servants to wait upon them! Andrew had travelled a long way since he had been born in that humble cottage in Dunfermline less than thirty miles from Kilgraston. One of their visitors wrote an amusing letter to her son.

Andrew Carnegie may be little, but his hoard and his heart are great, and he is a happy bridegroom indeed. Yesterday we returned from an excursion of two days to Dunfermline. As we returned in an opposite direction, we surprised all the servants dancing to the music of the pipes at the back of the house. They scurried to cover like rabbits, and when we drove round to the front door, there was the piper marching up and down playing " The Campbells are coming!" The butler, the housekeeper and the lady's maid were all waiting at the entrance, and all the housemaids were carrying hot water to the various bedrooms. It was the funniest transformation scene I ever saw.

Though, from now on, Andrew and his wife were to spend a great deal of their time in Scotland, he still kept his finger on the pulse of steel manufacturing in the United States. Every day cables were sent to him, telling him the output in tons of steel of each of his blast furnaces. He sent many long cables in reply giving detailed instructions. All this time more and more tons of steel were turned out from Carnegie's works. The demand for it was growing : it was needed not only for thousands of miles of railways, but for everything that had previously been made of iron. Factory machinery, farming implements, ships, boilers, axles and even nails were being made of steel. Factories and office buildings were built on steel frames. This was the beginning of the " Skyscraper " stage in the building of New York, when giant buildings of many storeys reached toward the skies. Most of these were built of Andrew Carnegie's steel. He had now made a tremendous fortune and was one of the wealthiest men in the world.

The thoughts of his great riches began to concern him very much. He had always held that a man should not possess great wealth just for his own benefit, but in trust to help mankind. He had never forgotten his dream of using his money to help others during his own lifetime. Still locked away in the little box of personal papers were the notes he had made twenty years earlier in which he had written, " Cast aside business for ever, except for others ", and the re-solve to spend the surplus of his money each year for benevolent purposes. The man was much older now but the dream remained. *He decided to give away his fortune before he died.*

Carnegie thought it was a very poor notion to leave money for charitable purposes when one was dead. He said that a rich man's life should be divided into two parts; first the acquiring of wealth; and second, the distributing of it among good causes. He wrote : " Rich men have it in their power during their lives to busy themselves in organizing benefactions from which the masses of their fellows will derive lasting advantage, and thus dignify their own lives."

The last paragraph of his writing ended, " The day is

138

not far distant when the man who dies leaving behind him millions of available wealth, which was free for him to administer during his life, will pass away ' unwept, un-honoured and unsung ', no matter to what uses he leave the dross he cannot take with him. Of such men people will say, ' *The man who dies thus rich, dies disgraced* '." Later on Andrew Carnegie was to set out these ideas in detail in a book he called *The Gospel of Wealth*.

In all these ideas his wife agreed entirely with Andrew. She gave him her help and enthusiasm in all he was doing, and when the copies of *The Gospel of Wealth* were pub-lished, she herself sent one to the man they both admired tremendously, whose friend they were proud to be, William Ewart Gladstone, the Prime Minister of Great Britain. With the book Mrs. Carnegie sent a letter.

Dear Mr. Gladstone,

We think we have found the true path—it is the one we mean to tread. If it commends itself to you we shall be so happy. Hoping you will find time to read it, and with every good wish for your prolonged health and happiness, in all of which you know my husband most heartily joins, believe me,

Most sincerely yours,

LOUISE W. CARNEGIE.

Mr. Gladstone was so delighted with it that he sent a cable asking permission to print part of it in the *Pall Mall Gazette*.

From now on both Andrew and Louise Carnegie were dedicated to the path they had chosen; the giving away of Andrew's tremendous fortune in the best way they could find to improve other people's lives. Andrew decided he would retire as soon as possible from business to give all his time to distributing his money, but before this could happen, a very sad thing occurred.

A serious strike took place at his largest steel works, the Homestead Works. In 1892 Carnegie appointed one of his

139

managers, Henry C. Frick, as the Chairman of the Carnegie Steel Company and gave him complete authority; then Andrew left to spend the summer in Scotland. New machinery and methods were introduced at the Homestead Works which enabled the steel-rolling men to earn half as much again as they had been doing, but the men were not satisfied with the wages offered. They demanded the whole of the extra profit the company was making should be paid to them in their wages.

Andrew Carnegie might have reached some agreement with his men, but he was in Scotland and was not even near a telegraph office at the time. Henry Frick was not a man to bargain with his work-people. Carnegie would have closed the works but told his men that their places were open to them when the dispute was settled. Not so Henry Frick! He dismissed the 218 rollers of steel, the company's most experienced men, and took on new men in their places. For fear of trouble Frick built a high board fence all round the works and stretched barbed wire along the top of it. Then it became known that he intended to employ a private army with guns, three hundred of them known as " Pinkertons ", to protect the works. When this was done he declared that the works would close on June 30, and that all the workmen would be discharged till they accepted his terms. If they wished to be taken on again they must apply as individuals and no member of any Union would be admitted.

A huge mass-meeting of angry work-people was held and the workers decided to seize the Homestead Works before the Pinkerton Guards could arrive. Henry Frick was certain that the arrival of the Pinkertons would settle the trouble, but the problem was how to get the guards into the works, for the strikers held every approach road. There was only one way—by the river.

The Homestead Works was built on the river bank. If the guards could be brought up the river by night, they could be smuggled into the works before the strikers were awake. Frick hired two barges, enough to bring three hundred Pinkertons from Pittsburgh.

Silently the barges crept along the river and a thick fog helped to hide them. About four a.m. they reached Homestead where the fog was dense indeed. All was quiet and the guards on the barges thought they would get into the works without being seen. Suddenly all pandemonium broke loose! Rockets were fired from the river banks, every steam whistle shrilled through the night, and bells were rung madly. The shout " The Pinkertons are here ! " went up in every street. Men, women and even children rushed from their beds and surged in a mob to the river bank. Yelling and shouting, they flung stones at the barges, then someone fired a pistol at the boats and other shots followed.

Still the barges came on up the river and made for the landing place. The howling mob made for it too, and over the wooden fence they poured, three thousand of them at least. The Pinkertons began to land from a gangway, carrying their rifles. The mob went mad with rage, and one of the strikers fired a pistol. In reply the guards fired a volley from their rifles. Five workmen were killed and many wounded, and three of the Pinkertons were also wounded to death.

The mob was stirred up by the firing to even greater fury. The strikers took up a position behind a barricade and shot away at every guard who attempted to cross the ground to the works. The Pinkertons fled to the barges again, the only shelter they could get.

For two hours the strikers fired at the barges, hurled dynamite at them, poured oil on the water and tried to set them on fire, but without success. At the end of two hours the firing slackened and the guards were invited to yield.

They agreed to go quietly away from Homestead if the strikers would give them safe conduct to the railway station.

This they agreed to do, and the Pinkertons came ashore and gave up their weapons. As they marched along to the railway station, however, the unarmed men were attacked by crowds of angry women who threw stones at them and set upon them with sticks, till the men managed to take refuge in a building, many of them desperately injured. The strikers were still in possession of the steel mills.

Three days later the Government sent eight thousand troops to Homestead to restore order. The strikers respected the Government army and gave up the steel-works again. The riot was over, though the strike was not settled for nearly three months after that, and after an attempt had been made to kill Frick, who was injured but escaped with his life.

Andrew Carnegie was on a coaching trip when Frick sent cables to him telling of the rioting and bloodshed, and these messages did not reach him till two days later. Of this sad business Carnegie wrote :

> Nothing I have ever had to meet in all my life, before or since, wounded me so deeply. No pangs remain of any wound received in my business career save that of Homestead. It was so unnecessary. The general public did not know that I was in Scotland and knew nothing of the trouble at Homestead. Workmen had been killed at the Carnegie Works of which I was the controlling owner. That was sufficient to make my name a by-word for years.

The first thing Carnegie did was to cable Frick that he was coming home by the first steamer he could take. This was the last thing Frick and his other partners wanted, for Andrew might have given in to the demands of his work-people. It would also have meant the end of Frick's career as general manager. Besides, the mischief had been done now, and nothing could alter what had happened, that blood had been shed. By cable Frick asked Andrew Carnegie not to return, and Andrew, seeing he could do no good by returning, decided to stay in Scotland. He had to support Frick, to whom he had given authority.

By the newspapers Carnegie was bitterly attacked for not returning and a deal of the trouble at Homestead was blamed on him. But Carnegie kept a dignified silence, and refrained from blaming Frick, though he knew in his heart that Frick's high-handed way of dealing with the affair had given him a bad name for the first time in his life as an employer.

In all this time of anxiety Louise gave great comfort and support to her husband. In a letter to William Gladstone about the strike Andrew said, " I have the support of a wife who is as strong and wise as she is gentle and devoted, so I shall sail on and let the tempest howl."

CHAPTER 9

The Dream Realized

FOR THE NEXT FEW YEARS ANDREW CARNEGIE'S LIFE WAS
a battle as far as his business was concerned. He and Henry
Frick were always having arguments that threatened to become quarrels. In the end Andrew Carnegie paid Frick his
share in the steel company and Frick left it.

There were other immense steel manufacturing firms in
the United States and competition between them became
very fierce indeed. Andrew began to feel that if he were
ever to retire from business he must sell his share in the Carnegie Steel Company. But who could afford to buy such
a vast concern and pay real money for it?

There was one man, one of Andrew's keenest rivals in the
steel business, John Pierpont Morgan, who possessed immense wealth too, and who wished to form a gigantic steel
company, the United States Steel Corporation. One of the
first steps he would need to take would be to buy up the
Carnegie Steel Company. He sent for Andrew Carnegie's
general manager, Charles Schwab, and during a long dis-
cussion that lasted all through the night, he asked Charles
Schwab, " Will Carnegie sell out? "

" I think he would," Schwab told him. " For the last ten
years he has said he would like to retire. If you offered him
a fair price for his Company, I think he would consider it."

" Well, if Andy wants to sell, I'll buy. Go and ask him
his price."

Schwab put the matter to Carnegie, who knew that he

would probably never get a better price than Pierpont Morgan would give him. After a further talk with Schwab he agreed to accept four hundred million dollars for the Carnegie Steel Company. That was over eighty million pounds! The bargain was sealed and Andrew Carnegie retired from the steel business on March 12, 1901.

The first thing Andrew Carnegie did with the money he received from the sale was to give four million dollars to the Homestead Works to provide an accident and pension fund. In his letter he said,

> I make this first use of surplus wealth on retiring from business as an acknowledgement of the deep debt I owe to the workmen who have contributed so largely to my success. It is designed to relieve those who may suffer from accidents, and provide small pensions for those needing help in old age.

Andrew always had the welfare of his workmen at heart.

The task of wisely using his surplus wealth began to take up all his time and attention. He took as his motto, " The gods send threads for a web begun." It was a motto particularly suitable for a weaver's son. He began his web with a gift of *sixty-eight* branch libraries for New York!

Just four years earlier great joy had come into Andrew Carnegie's life, the birth of his only child, a daughter. As he looked at the baby for the first time, Mrs. Carnegie said, " I would like her name to be Margaret, after your mother."

Andrew's cup of joy was full. No other name could have pleased him more, and for his dear wife to suggest it filled him with happiness.

" But I have a request to make," Mrs. Carnegie went on. " Now we have this little girl I would like to have a summer home for her. I don't want to have to rent one and be constantly going in and out. I want you to buy one for our own home."

Andrew Carnegie agreed at once.

" But I want to make one condition about it," Mrs. Carnegie said, smiling a little.

" What is that? "

" I want our summer home to be in the Highlands of Scotland."

" Bless you ! " Andrew Carnegie cried, delighted. " That suits me ! You know what Scotland means to me. A more understanding wife a man never had !"

At once Andrew Carnegie began to hunt for a Scottish castle he could buy. He wanted his castle to have everything that was delightful for a little growing girl; to be near the sea, to have its own stream and loch with a waterfall, and to have woods and hills within its grounds. At last he found all these things in Skibo, looking out on the lovely stretch of the Dornoch Firth.

The castle was in a very poor neglected condition, almost tumbledown. Andrew set to work at once to have it re-built, towers, pepperbox turrets, terraces and all, but it had modern comforts too, electric light and lifts ! There was also a swimming pool with heated water. Andrew built this castle specially for his wife and little daughter. Never even the dreams he had dreamed as a boy in Dunfermline and Allegheny had included such a wonderful castle as this !

It was a happy life that Andrew Carnegie lived at Skibo. Now he had time for yachting and fishing, walking and golf, and particularly writing. Here, too, he watched his dear little daughter grow up, and loved to tell her stories, many of them of his own making-up. Just as Uncle Lauder had taught him the ballads and songs of Scotland, so he now taught them to little Margaret. To him she was always " a wonderful wean." True happiness had come to Andrew Carnegie at last in his wife and child.

Many friends came to stay with them at Skibo Castle, including many famous people, authors, politicians, Members of Parliament, and even Cabinet ministers. One day a distinguished guest indeed came to visit Andrew Carnegie. He was the King of Great Britain, Edward VII.

King Edward was staying at Dunrobin Castle a few miles distant, and he was already on his way when the news was brought to Andrew Carnegie by telegram. He was having his usual afternoon sleep and was wearing the knicker-bocker suit he usually wore for the country life he lived. He jumped up, intending to change his suit for a more formal one, but already the King's car was coming up the drive. There was only just time for the piper to put on his kilt and get his pipes blowing to welcome His Majesty!

King Edward's visit lasted for more than an hour and Andrew Carnegie found him a pleasant, friendly guest. He was shown round the house and gardens and he much admired the swimming pool.

" I like the way you have built up this place, Mr. Car-negie," he said. " I hear that all your tenants and farmers have very good houses too. They all speak well of you as a landlord."

This praise warmed Andrew's heart. Then the King looked out of the window and saw a small girl, five years old, flitting about the flower beds and playing on the lawn.

" Is that your little daughter? " he asked Mrs. Carnegie.

" Yes, Your Majesty," Mrs. Carnegie smiled.

" I should like to see her," the King said at once.

As she brought her in, Margaret's governess gave her a hurried instruction how to greet the King, so that when Margaret arrived she gave a funny little ducking curtsey to His Majesty. King Edward was charmed with the delight-ful little girl.

" Won't you give me a kiss? " the King coaxed, bending towards her.

Margaret liked this elderly gentleman with a beard so like her father's, and at once she flung her ams round his neck and gave him a tremendous hug as well as a kiss.

"And now you must come and see my dolls," she insisted.

Quite willingly the King was led to the nursery and admired Margaret's family of dolls and was shown her other small treasures too.

As he was going away the King looked up at the tower and saw Andrew's rather unusual flag. It had the Stars and Stripes on one side and the Union Jack on the other.

"I like that idea," he said at once.

Margaret rushed up at that moment with two little posies of flowers in her hand. She had been busy gathering them.

"There is one for you," she said. "And here is one for you to take home to the Queen!"

"I'll put mine in my buttonhole now," King Edward declared, smiling.

King Edward was so much impressed by the wonderful work that Andrew Carnegie was doing for the benefit of his fellow men that he would have liked to give him a title. Andrew Carnegie, however, refused it, though he was grateful to the King. He looked on himself as a plain ordinary American citizen and he did not wish to change. Instead he said he would much rather have a letter from the King himself. King Edward wrote to him at once from Windsor Castle.

Dear Mr. Carnegie,

I have for some time past been anxious to express to you my sense of your generosity for the great public objects you have presented to this country, the land of your birth.

Scarcely less admirable than the gifts themselves is the great care and thought you have taken in guarding against their misuse.

I am anxious to tell you how warmly I recognize your most generous benefactions and the great services they are likely to confer upon the country.

As a mark of recognition I hope you will accept the portrait of myself which I am sending to you.

Believe me, dear Mr. Carnegie,

Yours sincerely,

EDWARD R. I.

All Andrew Carnegie's great gifts rose out of some human need in his own life. He never forgot his own desperate hunger for books, as a lad. That is what prompted his chief gift for the improvement of mankind, the free public library. Wherever a town was willing to pay for the books and upkeep of a library, Andrew Carnegie was willing to provide a fine building to house them.

As many as a thousand requests for libraries would come in during the year. At one point Andrew Carnegie said, " I am giving away libraries at the rate of two or three a day ! " He did not do this haphazardly. If he agreed that a library was necessary for a particular place, he would say what sum of money he was willing to give to build it, and his secretary had to see the plans of the building first. He spent over sixty million dollars (about twelve million pounds) on libraries. Nowadays the Town Councils are carrying on this wonderful work.

Andrew Carnegie was specially generous in his gifts to his birthplace, Dunfermline, and to Pittsburgh, where he had made his money in steel manufacture.

As a small boy he had often looked through the gates into Pittencrieff Glen that lay beside Dunfermline Abbey, or climbed a wall to get a better view of this lovely estate. He and other small boys had sometimes tried to sneak inside, but had always been chased away by the owner with his big dogs. Nearly every Sunday Uncle Lauder used to take Dod and Naig for a walk round the Abbey where they got a good view of the glen, and they used to wish they could walk in it freely. Alas, to them it was forbidden ground.

In Pittencrieff Glen stood the ruined tower of King Malcolm, St. Margaret's Cave and the tumble-down remains of the palace where King Charles I had been born. All these historic places belonged to one man, a Mr. James Hunt. It seemed wrong to Dunfermline people that these places, so famed in Scottish history, should not belong to the town, and that people should not be allowed to visit them freely. Andrew's uncle, the fiery Tom Morrison, was the leader of many disputes against Mr. Hunt, who, in a fit of anger, declared that " No Morrison or anyone kin to Morrisons shall ever set foot in Pittencrieff Glen."

Andrew used to look wistfully over the Abbey wall into the Glen and wish that small boys might play or wander in it. It was like paradise to him, but a forbidden paradise, for was he not " kin to the Morrisons "?

Over sixty years later it came to Andrew Carnegie's ears that the son of Mr. Hunt might be willing to sell the Glen and its historic places. There was no place on earth that Andrew Carnegie more wished to buy. He determined to possess it and offered Colonel Hunt forty-five thousand pounds for it, and Pittencrieff Glen became his.

" It always meant paradise to the child of Dunfermline," Andrew declared. " It certainly did to me. When I heard of paradise, I translated the word into Pittencrieff Glen, believing it to be as near paradise as anything I could think of. Happy were we if we caught a glimpse inside! "

It was then Andrew Carnegie had one of his happiest inspirations. He would make Pittencrieff Glen into a paradise. There the children should play on lovely green lawns and under the shady trees. There old people should sit in the sun and breathe the rose-scented air of the sunken gardens. There squirrels should climb and peacocks strut upon the terrace. He would give Pittencrieff Glen to Dunfermline, together with a great gift of money for its upkeep.

He handed over Pittencrieff Glen to the Carnegie Dunfermline Trust and with it funds that to-day bring in £48,000 a year. " All to be used in attempts to bring into the monotonous lives of the toiling people of Dunfermline more of sweetness and light, to give to them—especially the young—some charm, some happiness."

For over fifty years now the Carnegie Dunfermline Trust has faithfully followed Andrew Carnegie's directions. Pittencrieff Park and Glen is indeed a paradise for old and young, with its lovely gardens and greenhouses, ablaze with flowers; its playgrounds and lawns; its museum; its bright pavilion with a charming tea-room and a splendid concert hall. It has indeed brought " sweetness and light " to the folk of Dunfermline.

Andrew Carnegie also gave vast sums of money for education. It was his wish that every boy and girl who had sufficient intelligence should be able to go to a university, and that no student should be prevented because his parents could not afford to send him. Andrew Carnegie gave five million dollars (over a million pounds) to pay the class fees of students who could not afford to pay them. To this he added yet another million pounds to provide and equip libraries and laboratories; to help research and to provide scholarships for brilliant students to do research. For this he founded the " Carnegie Trust for the Universities of Scotland." To this Trust every deserving Scottish student in need of assistance to pay fees may apply.

During 1913 and 1914 Andrew Carnegie created the last of his great Trusts to carry on his work for mankind even after his death. This was the Carnegie United Kingdom Trust. To this he gave ten million dollars which brought in an income every year of over one hundred thousand pounds. This money was at first to be spent in providing public libraries, and in the encouragement of music, particularly by the gifts of church organs. Later on clinics and playing fields were provided. Everything was to be done to promote the advancement of knowledge and understanding among the people of the world.

It must be remembered that Andrew Carnegie gave similar gifts in the United States. He built the Pittsburgh Institute, and founded the Carnegie Corporation of New York to carry on his great work for the same purposes as the Carnegie United Kingdom Trust.

War was always a terrible and hateful thing to Andrew Carnegie. He never forgot the sad sights he had seen during the Civil War at the battle of Bull Run. He always hoped for an " International Court " to settle all quarrels between countries, without going to war.

He wrote himself,

> The day that the International Court is established will become one of the most memorable days in the world's history. It will ring the knell of man killing man—the deepest and blackest of crimes. It should be celebrated in every land as I believe it will some day, and that, perchance, not so remote as expected.

To help to make this dream of peace among nations come true, Andrew Carnegie built " The Peace Palace " at The Hague in Holland. There conferences could be held between nations to settle their differences peacably and here would be a library on international law. The cause of " Peace on earth, good will to men " became very dear indeed to Andrew Carnegie, for distrust seemed to be mounting between Britain and Germany. Andrew gave the last ten years of his life to try to make peace among nations. In 1910 he founded the " Carnegie Endowment for International Peace " and gave ten million dollars to it. In the gift letter he wrote that the money was " to hasten the abolition of international war, the foulest blot on our civilization . . . the crime of war is that it decides not in favour of the right, but of the strong."

In 1914 Andrew Carnegie, though nearly eighty years old, was as active and quick-spirited as ever. He was spending the summer with his family at Skibo Castle, and as usual they went to their house at Altnagar beside the River Shin. Often when they had few or no visitors, they spent a quiet restful time in this smaller house. It was while they were at Altnagar that the storms of war blew up over Europe. When Germany began to hack her way through Belgium towards France, Britain declared war on Germany. Andrew Carnegie's friends, knowing his great love for peace, felt that this blow might be too much for him if he learned of it suddenly in the newspapers. One of his very dear friends, the minister of Creich Parish, the Reverend Robert Ritchie, decided he had better break the news. He went to Altnagar, and, hot and distressed from hurrying, he asked to see Mr. Carnegie. Andrew sprang to his feet with his usual happy smile of welcome.

" Please sit down, Mr. Carnegie. I have sad news for you," Mr. Ritchie told him. " German armies have invaded Belgium and Britain has declared that unless they withdraw she will go to war."

Carnegie started, and his hand went to his breast. " Surely there's some mistake? Surely it can't be true? " he exclaimed, turning pale.

" I'm afraid it is only too true, Mr. Carnegie. Britain will be at war by midnight."

Andrew Carnegie looked like a man who had received a mortal blow. He jumped to his feet and paced up and down the room, utterly distracted.

" I can't believe it ! I can't believe it ! " he kept saying, then, as Mr. Ritchie shook his head sadly and the truth came slowly home to him, he cried, " Can't America do something to stop it? "

" I'm afraid that America is as powerless as Britain to make Germany turn back now," Mr. Ritchie said sadly.

Andrew Carnegie buried his face in his hands in terrible distress.

"All my castles in the air have fallen about me like a house of cards!" he declared.

It was plain that he was thinking of all his hard work for peace. The Carnegie Endowment for Universal Peace, the Peace Palace at The Hague, had all failed to prevent war. His dream of universal brotherhood was in shreds. He wrote that year, "The world convulsed by war as never before! Men slaying each other like wild beasts! I dare not relinquish all hope." In those last words speaks the great spirit of Andrew Carnegie, the man who would never give up hope, be the world unfaithful to his dream.

In mid-September of that fateful year the Carnegies returned to New York, and though for a while Andrew Carnegie took up his usual life at his house on Fifth Avenue, the war had dealt him a blow from which he never really recovered. He continued to give away what remained of his fortune, to the Red Cross, to the Y.M.C.A., to various organizations to help the sufferings of soldiers on the field of battle. Then, in February 1915, he had influenza, and after this illness he was never the same active man again and had to put aside all the activities in which he had taken such an energetic part. Though nursed well by his wife and his daughter, he gradually became weaker over the next few years. In August 1919 he was attacked by pneumonia again. At first he rallied. Two nights later, when he was settling down to sleep, his dear wife said, "Good-night, Andrew, I hope you will rest well", he replied gently, "I hope so, Lou, I hope so." He drifted into sleep, and from that quiet sleep Andrew Carnegie never woke again.

The things Andrew Carnegie had set out to do, he had done. He had gained a tremendous fortune but he had the greatness of soul to give it away to help mankind as he had promised he would. He had done this so wisely in his own lifetime that the good work would go on after his death, as it still goes on to-day. When he founded the Carnegie Corporation of New York he wrote :

My chief happiness as I write these lines lies in the thought that even after I pass away, the wealth that came to me to administer as a sacred trust for the good of my fellow men is to continue to benefit humanity for generations untold under the Trust's devoted and sympathetic guidance.

Andrew Carnegie's personal share in the work was finished. The pattern of his web, for which God had indeed sent threads, was now fully woven and complete.

But the work would go on.